The Freshwater Angler™

LIVE BAIT FISHING

Gunnar Miesen & Steve Hauge

CREATIVE
PUBLISHING
international

CHANHASSEN, MINNESOTA

www.creativepub.com

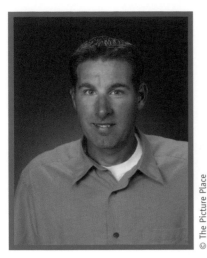

© The Picture Place

GUNNAR MIESEN is widely known for his ability to "root out" what the hot baits are for a particular area. Gunnar fishes for nearly all species of fish, but ranks large-mouth bass and steelhead as his favorites. He lives in Chaska, Minnesota.

© The Picture Place

STEVE HAUGE is a freelance editor and writer based in Savage, Minnesota, and has over 20 years in the fishing industry. Steve studied fisheries biology at the University of Wisconsin–Stevens Point. His favorite species to pursue are largemouth bass and muskies.

Copyright © 2005 by Creative Publishing international, Inc.
18705 Lake Drive East
Chanhassen, MN 55317
1-800-328-3895
www.creativepub.com

President/CEO: Michael Eleftheriou
Vice President/Publisher: Linda Ball
Vice President/Retail Sales & Marketing: Kevin Haas
Executive Editor, Outdoor Group: Barbara Harold
Creative Director: Brad Springer
Project Manager: Tracy Stanley
Photo Editor: Angela Hartwell
Director, Production Services: Kim Gerber
Production Manager: Stasia Dorn
Production Staff: Laura Hokkanen

Printed in China
10 9 8 7 6 5 4 3 2 1

LIVE BAIT FISHING
by Gunnar Miesen & Steve Hauge

Cover Photo: Bill Lindner Photography/blpstudio.com

Contributing Photographers: Gerald Almy, Denver Bryan, Jan Finger, F. Eugene Hester, Dwight R. Kuhn, Bill Lindner Photography, Gunnar Miesen, John E. Phillips, David J. Sams, Doug Stamm

Contributing Illustrator: Jon Q. Wright

Contributing Manufacturers: Alumacraft Boat Co., Berkely, Catfish Charlie's Bait Co., Inc., Cat Tracker Bait Co., Catcher Co./Smelly Jelly, Cortland Line Co., Inc., Frabill, Inc., Gambler Lures, Garmin, The Gapen Co., Kick'n Bass Products, Line Buster, Inc., Lowrance Electronics, Inc., Magic Bait Co., Inc., Marine Metal Products, P-Line, PowerPro, Uncle Josh Bait Company, Vexilar, Water Gremlin Co., Yum Bait Company

Library of Congress Cataloging-in-Publication Data

Miesen, Gunnar
    Live bait fishing / by Gunnar Miesen & Steve Hauge.
        p. cm. -- (The freshwater angler)
    Includes bibliographical references and index.
    ISBN 1-58923-146-5 (hardcover)
    1. Bait fishing. I. Hauge, Steven. II. Title. III. Series.
    SH455.4.M54 2004
    799.12'2--dc22
                                        2004003264

TABLE OF CONTENTS

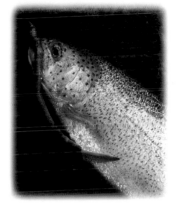

Introduction

For many people, including both of us, the earliest memories of fishing involve the use of live bait.

The scenarios may be different—angleworms under a bobber for bluegills, a lip-hooked shiner for largemouth bass or maybe it was your grandpa's favorite catfish bait recipe used to perfection. Whatever the case, the proper use of live bait is simply the best way to catch most species of freshwater fish.

Choosing the correct gear when you are getting started is one of the key components to angling success. In the pages of *Live Bait Fishing* we will take you through the basics of the equipment you will need to get started, no matter where you live. Whether you are a first-time angler or a seasoned veteran, you will find information that you can bring to your favorite reservoir, lake, river, stream or pond and have success from the very start. Many times, just going to the local bait shop and getting a scoop of minnows or a dozen worms is just not the best choice for success.

After you have the basic equipment knowledge, you will need to know which live baits are available to you, what they look like, where they live and how to catch and store them. Chapter 2 will cover all of these baits from worms to crayfish and frogs to leeches. It is often the freshest live bait that catches the most fish and we will show you how to keep yours in top form, with storage tips that are up-to-date, using the latest technology available.

We also included a chapter on scents and doughbaits. Although these are not considered traditional live bait, they are fished on many of the same rigs that you already use for live bait. In many instances these products can replace or enhance the live bait you are using to increase your catch. We also have brief commentary on pre-formed bait products that use scents to mimic live baits such as Berkley® PowerBait®. Again, these are not traditional live baits, but because they try to mimic scents of live baits they are fished in a manner closer to live bait than artificial lures. This chapter also includes some of our favorite doughbait and paste recipes for you to try.

In Chapter 4, we will take you through the details on how to catch all of the prominent fish species with easy-to-follow instructions on the best live-bait fishing techniques, with special tips to help increase your catch. We do this by following the yearly movements of each fish   from pre-spawn crappies in the spring, to catching walleyes through the ice in the winter. See how bait types and presentations change throughout the year as the fish change their feeding habits. Knowing where the fish are is just as important as what bait you use to catch them, and we will help you with where to look.

Finally, there are many different ways to get your live bait to the fish. It may be from the bank or several miles offshore in a boat. We have included tips for each of the main angling methods in the final chapter. Included is information on fishing from canoes, boats, float tubes, kick boats, shore fishing and wading. No matter what method you use to get your bait in the water, we will be there to help you along.

We hope that *Live Bait Fishing* helps you either begin your live-bait angling experience on the right foot, or increases your knowledge and improves your catch.

Gunnar Miesen & Steve Hauge

Chapter 1

Equipment

No matter what type of fishing you are going to pursue, having the proper equipment is essential to your angling success.

In recent years, technology and the increase of information available have offered anglers the best chances to catch greater numbers of fish. The increase in knowledgeable fishing pressure, however, has required anglers to use more of a finesse approach to catch fish in many cases.

Rods and Reels

Over the years, I have made a point to ask anglers I meet—whether it is at boat launches, fishing docks or piers—what they are fishing for. As you can imagine, I get many different responses to my question. The majority of the time the answer is the same: "Whatever bites."

Without even looking at the equipment used by the anglers who give me this common answer, I always get the same picture in my head. They are toting one push-button (spincast) reel on a 6-foot (1.8-m) medium-action rod spooled with 6- to 10-

Reel types include spincasting (top), spinning (middle) and baitcasting (bottom).

pound-test (2.7- to 4.5-kg) monofilament line, which has not been changed since it was purchased with the reel. If they are regulars to lakes, they often have one or two open-face (spinning) or baitcasting reels on 6- to 6 1/2-foot (1.8- to 2-m) medium- or medium-heavy action rods with 8- to 12-pound-test (3.6- to 5.4-kg) monofilament.

Other than using old line, this is exactly the type of equipment I recommend for anglers who enjoy the excitement and fun of not knowing what might be on the other end of the line each time they set the hook.

Many anglers have certain species of fish they like to target, which often requires specialized equipment. The rod, reel and line size should match the size and species of fish you are after, the bait you are using and the type of structure you are planning to fish.

Rod lengths from 6 to 7 1/2 feet (1.8 to 2.3 m) are standard when live-bait fishing; shorter rods work best for short casts and in limited space situations. Longer rods work best when you are trying to cast longer distances, fight larger fish, or are in a boat.

Most rods come with a rating that ranges from ultralight to

extra-heavy. This designation refers to the power of the rod or, in general terms, how much the rod will bend when pressure is applied. The heavier the power, the less the rod will bend. Rod manufacturers also use the term action, which describes how quickly the rod begins to bend at the tip. Actions range from slow, which has an almost parabolic bend, to extra-fast, where only the tip of the rod bends.

Matching your reel to the rod simply means that you have enough line capacity on the reel to hold the correct-size line needed to properly present your live-bait rig to the fish. It should also be the correct weight to balance well on the rod you've chosen, and be built strong enough to get the fish out of cover.

The best line size depends on the structure found in the area of the fish you are after. Most of my live-bait fishing is done with 6- to 10-pound-test (2.7- to 4.5-kg) monofilament line and is strong enough to fight fish up to 7 or 8 pounds (3 to 3.6 kg), yet light enough to still present a natural-looking live-bait rig.

Push-button or closed-face reels are best for beginners and can be used for most types of fishing with live bait. A spinning, or "open face," rod and reel allow more advanced anglers to cast smaller live-bait rigs farther. Spinning reels also have a much better drag than most push-button reels, which is critical when fishing with light line.

One of my many fishing mentors gave me some advice that I

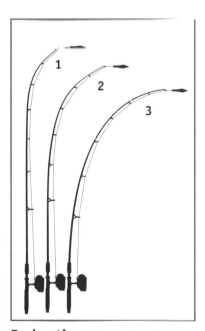

Rod action is shown by pulling equally on different rods of the same power. A fast-action rod (1) bends mainly near the tip; a medium-action (2), over the front half; and a slow-action (3), over the entire rod length.

repeat to myself every time I prepare to go on a fishing trip: Never leave the house without a 6-foot (1.8-m) spinning rod spooled with 8-pound-test (3.6-kg) line. Over the years, that 6-foot spinning rod and reel has come in very handy in many different situations.

Baitcasting, or "levelwind," rod and reel combinations are a must when chasing larger fish with live bait. Baitcasters give you the ability to cast larger live-bait rigs, fish with heavier line, allow for greater line capacity and have smoother drag systems. Baitcasters also work great for trolling live bait because the line does not twist as much as it can with a spinning or push-button reel when reeling into a moving boat.

Bobbers

Whatever name you use—bobber, cork or float—understanding the importance of this tool is vital to a successful fishing trip. Bobbers, as I call them, provide the ability to cast live bait farther, suspend the bait at the depth the fish are located and detect fish strikes. They also allow you to utilize wind and wave action to cover more water, and give live bait more action.

The depth of water you fish determines whether a fixed bobber or sliding bobber is best. I often fish a fixed bobber in depths of 5 feet (1.5 m) or less, simply because it is very difficult to safely cast a

bobber rig with more than 5 feet of line below the bobber. A sliding or "slip" bobber slides down your line until it hits the first sinker or the hook itself and allows you to cast with ease. This is the preferred style of bobber when fishing deep water. With sliding bobbers, the depth of your bait can be adjusted by raising or lowering the bobber stop, which is simply a knot that slips onto the line before the bobber is threaded on. It is set at the desired depth to keep the bait in proper position.

The biggest mistake I see anglers make is that they select a bobber that is too big. Although being able to see your bobber is very important, using a bobber that is too big results in fewer fish at the end the day. A 1-inch (2.5-cm) bobber, for instance, floats a small split-shot (size B or BB) and a #8 or #10 hook with a fathead minnow attached. Regardless of the size of bobber you're using, a rule of thumb is to have no more than half of the bobber showing above the waterline. The bobber still has good visibility and it reduces the resistance felt by the fish when taking the bait.

Today, there are many different shapes of bobbers, each designed for different purposes. The trend set by bobber manufacturers is that of cylinder shapes. This style of bobber has less water resistance when a fish moves off with the bait. You no longer need to rely only on the round, red-and-white bobber. Most good tackle shop employees should be able to help you choose the best bobber for your application.

Popular bobber styles include: (1) glow, (2) lighted, (3) weighted, (4) antenna and (5) balsa, (6) heavy current, (7) spring-lock and (8) round plastic.

Popular sinker styles include: (1) egg, (2) bell, (3) walking, (4) bullet, (5) bank, (6) pyramid, (7) rubbercore, (8) bead chain, (9) split-shot, (10) Bait-Walker, (11) bottom bouncer.

Sinkers

Like bobbers, sinkers come in two styles: fixed and sliding. Fixed sinkers work best when your bait is suspended under a bobber or trolled above the bottom. The benefits of a sliding version—called a slip-sinker—on or near the bottom is that when a fish takes the bait, you can feed it line and the sinker will rest on the bottom allowing the fish to take the bait without feeling any resistance. This is possible because the line slides freely through the sinker. Many times, inactive or pressured fish drop a bait before inhaling the hook if there is too much resistance from the sinker.

Water depth, bottom structure and the speed the bait will be traveling are the determining factors of the size and type of sinker to use. Remember to use just enough weight so that no more than half the bobber is above the waterline.

The shape of a sinker is as important as the size. Here are a few examples:

• Bullet-shaped sinkers work best in weeds or brush.

• Egg-sinkers should be used when fishing on the bottom in sand, gravel or rocky areas when drifting or trolling. Egg-sinkers also work well on slip-sinker rigs that are fished on the bottom.

Non-Lead Sinkers

An estimated 3 million pounds (1.35 million kg) of lead sinkers are lost in our rivers, streams and lakes each year by anglers. Experts feel that switching to non-lead fishing products will curb any permanent damage to our watery playgrounds. Lead is most dangerous to young anglers; because children's bodies are still developing, even small amounts of lead absorbed through the skin may have an effect on them in later years.

The ban on lead fishing products has been a reality for some states in the South and East, with other states to follow suit in the near future. Sinker manufacturers have been working for the last few years to develop lead-free alternatives. Zinc, tin, bismuth and tungsten have been the primary alternatives to lead. These materials produce a more refined sinker in appearance. The trade-off, however, is that they are often a little bigger and more costly than lead.

- Bottom-bouncers are sinkers best used when trolling live-bait rigs and you want to keep them on the bottom. They allow you to cover large pieces of structure because the design of a bottom-bouncer helps keep live-bait rigs up off the bottom and free from snags.
- Casting sinkers with a built-in swivel are used with many popular live-bait rigs, such as the paternoster rig.
- Pyramid sinkers look just like their name would suggest, with the pointed top having a built-in brass loop used to attach the sinker to the line. The design of a pyramid sinker allows it to hold better when fishing heavy current or wave action with a live-bait rig.

When trolling, the speed and depth you want your bait to travel determines the size of sinker to use. The deeper and faster you fish, the more or heavier sinker you need.

Fishing line creates drag (resistance) when moving through the water and raises the bait as you increase the speed. When the bait is in contact with the bottom, as when drift-fishing for walleyes, it is very important to use enough weight so you can feel any change in the terrain. But be careful not to use so much weight that you end up dredging the lake deeper.

On a recent walleye trip, it became clear that by choosing the right sinker while drifting, we were able to determine where the harder sand was in the area we were fishing. We caught more fish because we just keyed in on these areas of harder sand, which were so subtle that we were not able to consistently spot the changes in bottom on our graph. Fish often relate to bottom changes.

Lines

Over the past ten years manufacturers have been working with anglers and scientists to design a new generation of fishing line. Understanding the benefits of each type will streamline your decision-making process when you're at the store or ordering on-line.

When I worked at a tackle shop in high school we offered just the basics: the old standby extra-tough monofilament for baitcasters, extra-limp monofilament for spinning reels and Dacron, primarily for use on baitcasting reels for big fish. We also sold spools of cheap (no-name) line for anglers who fished only occasionally.

Fishing line was also much more cost effective in those days; the store would have a line sale each year when we would sell and wind line on the customer's reel for a penny per yard. Today you don't easily find shops that offer line winding, even for expensive line.

The one thing that has not changed is the number of anglers I see fishing with line that appears to be many years old and probably came with the reel when it was first purchased. That's not a good way to fish. Remember that your line is the only connection between you and the fish— it should be a good connection.

Monofilament

This line is still the king as far as sales, but even mono has been separated into sub-categories to meet specific fishing situations. The most common areas of advancement touted by manufacturers are: low diameter, low stretch, low memory, color, increased knot strength and abrasion resistance.

I like the low-diameter lines that allow more line to fit on smaller, lightweight reels. They make it possible to use lighter-weight sinkers because thin line has less water resistance.

Low-stretch line is great for fishing deep water or casting long distances, as with a slip-bobber or slip-sinker rig. You get a better hook set and better sensitivity with this line type.

Low-memory is a feature that comes with lots of hype. In my experience, after sitting on a reel for extended periods, most mono has too much memory.

As far as colors are concerned, I believe clear and green are all that are needed. The rest probably just cause confusion for the angler.

Knot strength in the new mono lines is greatly improved and has made a large impact in the fishing world. Too many anglers hurry through tying knots as if it were a race, breaking more line than they should. These new monos help that.

All fishing lines have increased abrasion-resistance characteristics. The amount of abuse they take has helped a lot more anglers catch fish. I oftentimes have to plead with people I fish with to check and retie their line while out fishing. I suspect the number of fish lost due to nicked and frayed fishing line is huge. It's my second biggest pet peeve (having dull hooks is the first!).

Dacron

This well-known line is still out there with some subtle changes that have improved it, but it really has taken a backseat to the new braids.

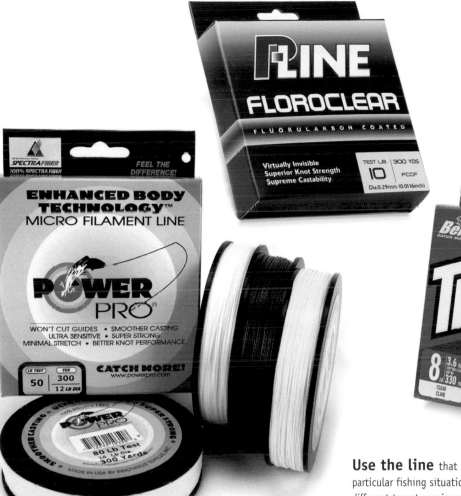

Use the line that works for you in your particular fishing situation. Different rigs and different target species will make opportunities for using a variety of line types.

Braids and Superlines

Most good anglers I know have experimented with several different brands before finding the one that fits their needs and fishes the way they want.

True braids are made by tightly weaving small diameters of Spectra® fiber into a continuous line, which is then coated with some type of temporary color or wax to give it stiffness and angler appeal.

Superlines are braids that have been heat or chemically fused, then coated with temporary color or wax for angler appeal.

Both have very little stretch, great abrasion resistance and good knot strength when tied with a Palomar knot or Duncan loop. Braids and superlines also have low diameters for their strength. They both excel when trolling, fishing heavy cover and fishing deeper water. They also greatly increase the sensitivity you feel through the rod.

Fluorocarbon

This is a newer concept in fishing line, designed to refract less light in water, making it appear nearly invisible to fish. Fluorocarbon is used mainly as leader material and has super

strength and great abrasion resistance. It has become my top choice in clear water or when fishing for walleye, trout, steelhead, salmon or small-mouth and largemouth bass.

Most of the early manufacturers of low-grade fluorocarbon are out of business and you can feel confident to try it again if your first go-round was not a pleasant one.

If fluorocarbon seems expensive, that's the good stuff in most cases and you should buy it. Fluorocarbon does require you to tie a good knot—and remember to wet the line before cinching down the knot.

Three Easy Knots for Attaching Hooks, Terminal Tackle and Line

The Palomar Knot is easy and fast to tie and handy for attaching hooks, swivels and other terminal tackle to your fishing line. It is especially popular with anglers using braided fishing lines. (1) Double about 6" (15 cm) of line and pass through the eye of the hook. (2) Tie a simple overhand knot in the doubled line, letting the hook hang loose. Avoid twisting the lines. (3) Pull the end of the loop down, passing it completely over the hook. (4) Pull both ends of the line to draw up the knot. Trim excess.

The Trilene Knot is one of the easiest knots for novice anglers to learn how to tie. Experts also like the knot because it can be easily tied at night in complete darkness. (1) Slide your line through the hook eye, and repeat, entering the line from the same direction and being sure to form a double loop at the hook eye. (2) Wrap the tag end around the standing line four or five times, moving away from the hook. (3) Pass the tag end back through the double loop at the hook eye, moisten, pull the knot tight against the hook eye, and trim the tag end (4).

The Blood Knot works great for splicing two lines of similar diameter. (1) Cross the two sections of line to be joined, and then wrap one tag end around the standing part of the other line five to seven times, depending on line diameter. (2) Pass the tag end back between the two lines. (3) Wrap the other tag end in the same manner, and bring it back through the same opening. (4) Pull the standing lines to tighten knot; trim.

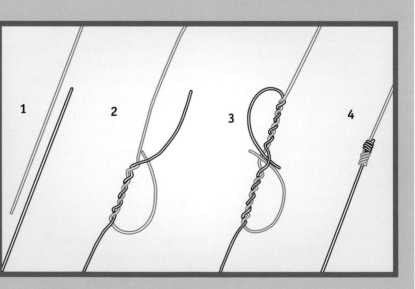

Hooks

With so many shapes and sizes of hooks, how do you select the right one for your situation? Here are the factors I take into consideration: size of the fish's mouth, type of structure this fish lives around and size and type of live bait I plan to use.

The hook you select should be big enough so the point protrudes through the bait by about 1/8 inch (3.2 mm). For open-water situations, I like a lighter wire hook, which makes for better hook penetration when setting the hook. In heavy cover like weeds, brush piles or rocks, I like a heavy wire hook that allows more pressure to be put on the fish when setting the hook and hauling it out. The thicker wire also keeps a sharper hook point and does not have as much of a tendency to straighten out.

The most common hook types used for live-bait fishing can be divided into five categories:

• Live-bait hooks are typically designed with a wide gap and shorter shank. This gives the hook a small profile.

• Long-shank hooks have a smaller gap and an extra-long shank and are used for fish with smaller mouths, which is common to many of the panfish species.

• Bait-keeper hooks have a standard length shank, and feature small barbs that help secure the live bait to the hook, reducing the chance of smaller fish stealing your bait.

• Khale-style hooks, with their odd design, hold a baitfish securely and are designed with an oversize gap for positive hook penetration.

• Treble hooks feature three hooks that are welded together to create one hook. Having three hook points increases the hooking percentages, especially when fishing with larger baitfish.

There have been great advances in recent years when it comes to the metals and finishes used by hook manufacturers. Many hooks are sharper than

they have ever been and they come in several fish-attracting colors. Premium hooks come with higher price tags but the confidence I get from tying on a premium hook with a good knot to fresh line is priceless.

Even so, I still find myself using a standard bronze-finished hook when fishing from shore and in snag-filled areas. In those instances, there is a lack of mobility to retrieve my live-bait rig once it's snagged. In the end, using a premium hook would just not be cost effective.

Specialized hooks have been around for several years and when used in the right situations they make a big difference. The most recent specialty hook to come on the scene is the circle hook, pioneered in the saltwater markets; circle hooks have made their way into the freshwater market with great success.

The design of a circle hook came from the quest to find a hook that would help solve the problem of fish swallowing the hook completely. This often

Popular hook syles include: (1) treble, (2) octopus, (3) Kahle, (4) O'Shaughnessy, (5) live bait, (6) baitholder, (7) circle, and (8) weedless.

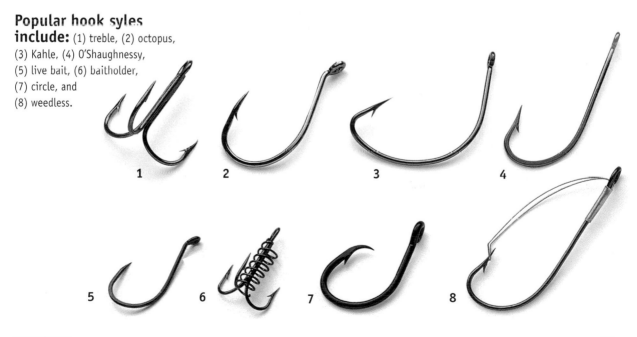

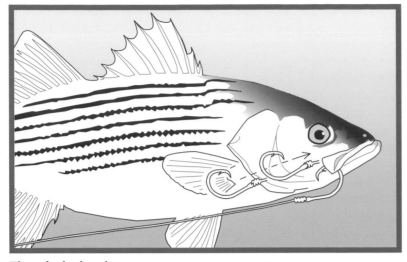

The circle hook is designed to penetrate the outside corner of the jaw.

Sharpening

Over the years I have conditioned myself to frequently check the sharpness of my hook.

Even if I take a new hook straight from the package I still check the sharpness of the hook point by gently scraping it over my thumbnail. If the hook point does not grab my thumbnail with very little pressure, I reach into my tackle bag and use one of the three hook sharpeners I carry with me at all times.

Although the hooks on the market today are very sharp and hold a point well, many factors can play a role in dulling them. The following are the most common factors contributing to a dull hook: the hard bones in a fish's mouth, rocks, gravel, wood and assuming a new hook is sharp when it's not.

When fishing with live bait, a sharp hook point allows you to penetrate the bait with little effort so as not to crush or damage it before it has a chance to catch the big one for you.

forced anglers to cut the line and release the fish hoping it would live, or keep an unwanted fish because it was hooked so deeply. Circle hooks are designed to allow anglers to let the fish swallow the hook and bait as they normally would. When it is time to set the hook, however, anglers should simply begin reeling with constant pressure on the fish. The hook then travels from deep inside the fish's mouth until it reaches the outside corner where it actually penetrates while trying to come free.

One thing that most anglers do not do as often as they should is pinch down the barb on their hooks. I don't think you'll lose many more fish than you would with the barb in its original position. Any timesaver is very important. Not only does pinching down the barb on a hook allow you to unhook fish faster, it also allows for easier hook penetration and causes less harm to the fish.

Sharpening Hooks

Flatten the outside edge of the point using a hook file (near right). Begin filing at the barb and work toward the point of the hook.

File one side of the point, beginning at the barb (middle). Remove enough metal so the side is flat and slanted toward the inside of the point.

Turn the hook and file the other side of the point in the same manner (far right). When completed, the point should be three-sided.

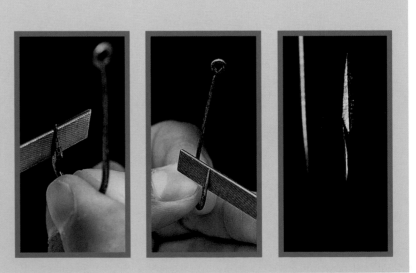

Electronics

From an early age I realized the important role electronics play in many fishing situations. Modern technology has given anglers the ability to locate fish and structure; determine depth, surface temperature and trolling speed; and, most recently, record and store the location of their favorite fishing spots.

You can rely on the following popular electronics to increase your fishing success.

• Flashers allow anglers to get a quick reference of depth. They also mark structure and fish. When fishing shallow water, heavy weed growth or through the ice I prefer to use a flasher. Flashers also work well as portable units because they require less battery power to operate, so they can often run for days without wearing down your battery.

• Liquid-crystal recorders, called LCRs for short, are the most common electronics used by anglers today. The LCR's television-like screen shows more detail than a standard flasher unit. Today's high-tech LCRs are nothing short of personal computers, making them very easy to use and understand. I rely on an LCR unit for deeper, open-water fishing; searching a large area looking for structure; or when trolling or drifting suspended fish.

• Global positioning systems, commonly known as GPS, give anglers the ability to record and store many different spots they fish and return to them time after time, even year after year. GPS units use satellites to triangulate speed, direction of travel and position on earth.

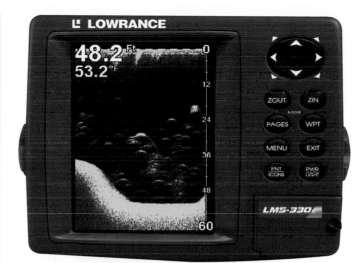

Electronics come in different sizes, shapes and price ranges, depending on what your budget is and what you want to use them for. Shown here are an LCR (top), flasher (above), and GPS (right).

Many LCR units can be purchased with a built-in GPS. Portable GPS units are also sold separately, called hand-helds.

• Underwater cameras are the ultimate in marking structure and fish. All the time spent looking down a hole in the ice gave a group of Midwesterners the idea to develop the ability to get an up-close look at objects under the water's surface without getting wet, in summer or winter. You now have the ability to identify fish species and structure—even find lost items. I have used an underwater camera for several years and find the entertainment and educational value priceless.

Unfortunately, even with the vast number of electronics available to anglers today, it doesn't mean the fish are going to bite. But sometimes just a little extra help is all you need!

Chapter 2

Live Baits

The simple fact that fish in every lake, river, pond and reservoir already feed on bait to survive makes your job of trying to catch them considerably easier.

What we have to do as anglers is to determine which types of bait are most prevalent in the waters we are fishing, catch them, and then try to present them to the fish in such a fashion that causes them to bite. Hopefully, we can even enhance the bait to actually increase its appeal to the fish.

Baitfish

Although there are many kinds of small fish to use as bait, most anglers lump them together and call them all "minnows." To many anglers, picking the correct one is a very serious decision that has to be made before heading out to the lake, stream or river. I spent ten years selling minnows and tackle to these anglers and, for many of them, it was not an easy decision. With 250 species of minnows in North America there's good reason to spend time narrowing the options. Minnows are the number-one live bait used by anglers pursuing their favorite fish species.

The following are key points to consider when deciding which species is the best one to purchase at your local bait dealer.

Hardiness

This is something that takes a bit of research on your part, but once you have a basic understanding of which species are hardy and which ones may need extra attention, your "dead bait" days will be over. Having lively bait on the end of your line may make the difference between catching fish and coming home empty-handed. With advances in aeration systems and water-treatment chemicals, keeping most baitfish alive is now possible.

Certain species of baitfish are definitely hardier than others and knowing which one to purchase in the first place helps. Most bait shop owners will give you a straight answer when it comes to which live bait is working best for that area.

Whenever possible I highly recommend examining the shop's bait tanks to check for healthy-looking bait before you purchase. If your local dealer does not sell large quantities of bait be sure to ask about the delivery schedule so you can get the freshest bait possible.

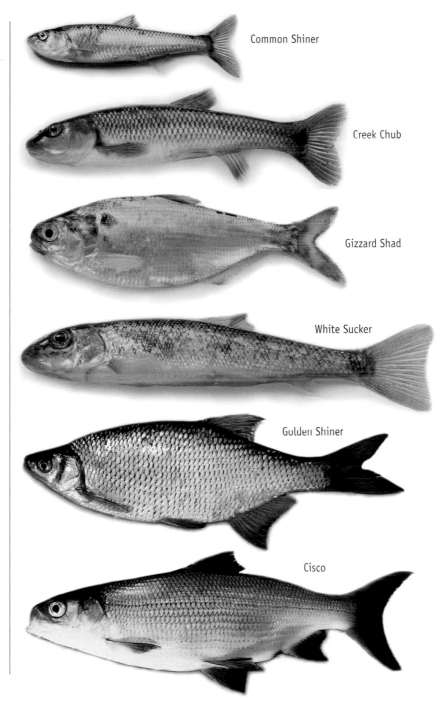

Common Shiner

Creek Chub

Gizzard Shad

White Sucker

Golden Shiner

Cisco

Hardiness Chart

EXTREMELY HARDY	MODERATELY HARDY	SOMEWHAT HARDY	LEAST HARDY
American Eel, Fathead Minnow, Madtom, Mudminnow	Blacknose Dace, Bluegill, Bluntnose Minnow, Creek Chub, Finescale Dace, Goldfish, Horny-head Chub, Mottled Sculpin, Southern Redbelly Dace, White Sucker	Banded Killifish, Common Shiner, Golden Shiner, Red Shiner, Yellow Perch	Alewife, Cisco, Emerald Shiner, Gizzard Shad, Rainbow Smelt, Spottail Shiner

Size

Select the size of your bait to match the size of lure you use or try to match the size of the minnows you've seen in the water. Be careful not to use bait that your equipment is not set up for.

Use a larger-than-average bait if smaller gamefish are around and you are having problems with them picking off pieces of your bait before it can attract bigger fish. When fishing for heavily pressured fish, choosing smaller baitfish is better in most cases. You can also downsize your minnows when fishing clear water, and increase the size for stained water.

Here's the timetable I use when thinking about bait size:

• Early in the season, I actually use slightly larger bait because most of the bait in the system have grown over the winter and are adults that were born the previous year.

• After the spawn, I downsize my bait choices, as most waters are filled with young-of-the-year baitfish.

• As the year progresses I steadily increase the size of my bait as the baitfish in the system grow.

These are just a few general rules, but if you keep an eye on the size of the baitfish you see in the water, the better your chances are for success.

Shape

Most fish have mouths that are better suited for eating long, thin baitfish like a fathead minnow or sucker species. These baitfish tend to have less fish-attracting "flash" than a deeper-bodied baitfish like shiners or baby sunfish and crappies.

Oxygen-pack baitfish for a long trip. Some bait shop operators will put the fish in plastic bags filled with water and pure oxygen. The fish will last for several days.

Fish blessed with bigger mouths, such as largemouth bass, striper, catfish or larger pike and walleye, are much better suited to handle deeper-bodied baitfish. I believe in the old fishing adage "Big bait, big fish." And I keep it in mind as I choose my bait for each outing.

Color

Even though most baitfish tend to be neutral in color, there are some species that have brightly colored scales. For example, shad and shiner species often have silver or gold scales. The reason is that species that tend to travel in schools, near the top of the water column, use the silver coloring to confuse other fish chasing the school.

The flashing in different directions from fleeing bait causes confusion in the predator fish and leads to the survival of the prey group. I like to change between silver and golden shiners and let the fish tell me which one they prefer. Always try to bring several

minnow species along when you are going fishing, so you have the option of changing.

Some species have brightly colored stripes or bars along their bodies, which also can be an attraction factor. Again, it's just figuring out what the fish are feeding on and matching it as closely as you can with your bait.

Scent

The scent of a baitfish can also be a very important factor in attracting fish with live bait. For some species, such as catfish that often feed at night, scent is used almost exclusively to catch them. Obviously, you can't ask for a certain minnow that "smells" more than another species. What you can do, as with catfish or big coldwater pike, is puncture the bait slightly or scrape off a section of the scales to allow more of its scent to escape and give off the smell of an injured baitfish. You can also use store-bought scents to make your bait more appealing.

Catching and Keeping Baitfish

Because some very productive baitfish will not survive the stress of being held for several days in a commercial minnow tank at the bait shop, anglers must catch these baitfish— sometimes daily—before or after they go out fishing to be prepared for the next outing. Options are using traps, a variety of nets and a hook and line.

Traps

Trapping is the most common method because it is the simplest and causes the least amount of damage to the baitfish. I recommend purchasing commercial traps, which are available at most bait shops.

Simply bait the trap with bread or crackers and set it in shallow water with a sandy bottom. I usually set my traps in the morning and check them after the sun has gone down. Marking your traps well is very important to save time in finding them in the dark.

If you are trapping in a stream or river be sure to secure your trap well so it cannot be swept away by the current when it fills up with bait.

Seines

Seining is a little more difficult than trapping because it requires two people, in most cases, and waders. One pass, however, with a seining net could yield enough baitfish for a whole weekend of fishing.

Seining nets are sold at most tackle shops and range in price and size. I use a 20-foot-long by 4-foot-deep (6- by 1.2-m)

Trapping minnows

Snap apart the trap and bait it with a few pieces of bread or crackers. In muddy water, attach a marker. In a stream, add rocks to the trap so the current will not move it.

Set the trap in shallow water. Leave it for several hours or overnight.

Seining is most productive in shallow water. Backwaters, small streams and lake or river shorelines usually hold many baitfish. Pull the seine with the outside seiner moving ahead of the person near shore. This keeps many baitfish from swimming around the end of the net.

net, with floats on the top and lead weights on the bottom to ensure the net is dragging the bottom and the baitfish are not sneaking out underneath.

I use plastic zip-ties to affix two broom handles 5 feet (1.5 m) in length to each side of the seine. We position one person close to shore and the other out no deeper than 3 feet (1 m). The person closest to shore remains stationary while the person on the other end of the net walks to shore in a half-circle path, keeping the net tight at all times.

Remember: Moving too fast will allow the lead weights to lift off the bottom, resulting in lost baitfish.

Cast Nets

My first experience with cast nets came when I was on a photo shoot on Lake Cumberland in Kentucky. We needed fresh shad because we found that if we didn't catch our bait the night before each day of fishing we wouldn't catch as many fish.

Cast nets work best for baitfish that school near the surface and can be used by one person. Locating and attracting these schools can be done at night with lights or by baiting them with crackers or bread.

The art of throwing a cast net requires practice but the allure of catching a 25-pound (11-kg) striper was enough to get me to master it quickly! We purchased a 12-foot (3.6-m) net at the local bait shop and school was in session. The object was to get the net to land out over the school of baitfish while completely opening up to its 12-foot-diameter (3.6-m) circle.

Using a Cast Net

Hold the weighted line with the other hand and your teeth. Hoist the net into the water. It should open into a big circle, and the weights pull it down to surround the fish.

Tie the retrieving line of the net to your wrist and, with the same hand, grasp the net where it is attached to the line.

Pull the line to draw the net shut and retrieve the baitfish.

Umbrella and Dip Nets

Both of these types of net can be operated by a single angler and work best when you are trying to catch minnows that gather in small areas, like an eddy in a stream or around docks and piers.

Umbrella nets are lowered to the bottom and let sit, while you try to attract a school of baitfish with crackers or bread. When the school of baitfish is tightly bunched up, quickly pull the net up from the bottom and catch as many as you can.

Dip nets have a smaller hoop size than a standard gamefish net and the size of the mesh is also smaller so baitfish cannot swim right through it. Dip nets have distinctively long handles of at least 6 feet (1.8 m), which allows anglers to reach out farther. Once you have located a school of baitfish, simply sweep the net down, through the school and back up to the surface. Most dip netters have the best luck right before and after dark, which allows anglers to get closer to the schools without spooking them.

Hook and Line

This is by far the most exciting way to catch baitfish, in my opinion. In most cases, the trick is that it requires using smaller tackle. Large shiners, chubs, shad and suckers are some good hook-and-line candidates.

I prefer to use an ultralight spinning outfit, flyrod or cane pole to catch baitfish. Pinching down the barb on a small hook, size #12 or #14, will result in less damage to the baitfish when you're unhooking them.

Bait your hook with a small doughbait, worm or insect

Dip nets work best in shallow rivers and streams, or from docks along lakeshores. Many species of baitfish, such as smelt, can be dipped more easily at night.

Hook-and-line angling is a whole other sport in itself. Remember to handle the baitfish carefully and try to remove the hook without tearing its mouth. You can use corn, breadballs, pieces of worm, insects or artificial flies and lures. If you don't have a small lure, tie some red thread to a tiny hook.

larvae. Small panfish jigs and nymph flies also work well. With fish like suckers, or when fishing a slight current as you would for chubs, some small split-shot may be used to get the bait down to where the fish are. In many parts of the country, multiple-hook rigs are legal—and used often.

Aeration

If you are a frequent baitfish angler, one of the easiest ways to keep your bait hardy is to invest in some type of aeration system. Ultimately, having a good aeration system saves time and money, and results in more time on the water. No

more running to the bait shop every day or waking up to a bucket full of dead minnows.

Systems range from adding simple oxygen tablets to the water, to using portable 12-volt oxygen-generating units.

If you spend most of your time fishing on the bank several inexpensive, battery-operated models are available. If you fish out of a boat that does not have a bait well, models designed to run off the 12-volt battery already in your boat work well. Here's a tip: You can simply take a small cooler and install a recirculating pump system in it that runs off a small closed-cell 12-volt battery.

Flow-through bait buckets work well while fishing in the cooler temperatures of spring and fall or when trolling. As water and air temperatures increase during the summer, however, aeration systems are a must to protect your investment. They are also a must for keeping bait overnight or until the next time you go fishing.

Fresh water along with aeration keep your bait fresh for extended periods of time. When fresh lake water is not accessible make sure to use purified or well water instead. Most tap water contains too many treatment chemicals harmful to many types of live bait.

Types of containers and equipment

for keeping minnows alive include portable bait buckets (below) with aerators that run off a 12-volt battery or alkalines; or large containers (left) for storing larger quantities of bait for longer periods of time.

Worms and Leeches

"Worms" are by far the most widely used live bait in North America, simply because they are readily available at bait shops and are very easy to catch and keep. Hundreds of species are found throughout the continent. They all have a similar shape and are usually referred to as "earthworms."

Also found throughout North America are leeches—in lakes, ponds, marshes and slow-moving streams. Deep brown in color, the most distinctive feature on leeches is their sucking disks, one of which appears on each end of the body. The small sucking disk is the head end, used for eating. The large sucking disk end is the actual tail, which is used to cling to objects while the other end eats.

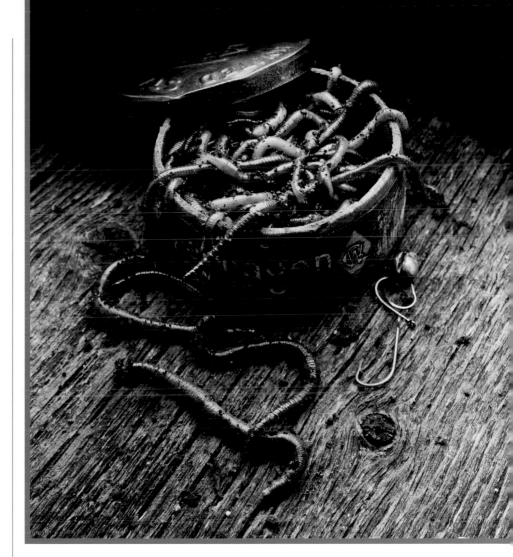

Worms

Earthworms consume enough soil to equal their weight every 24 hours, leaving a fertilizing trail of humus (worm poop) in their wake. Some people are not aware that this humus is critical for healthy lawns and gardens, as it frees valuable minerals from the soil and aerates root systems.

Earthworms are very sensitive to light, which makes night the best time for catching these wiggling creatures. Many earthworm species feed on the surface at night by leaving just their tail section anchored in their burrow underground. Feeding in this position allows for a quick getaway should they become spooked and hurry backward down the hole.

Worms mate by lying next to each other as their eggs are fertilized through the skin, giving birth two to three weeks later. While mating, worms cannot react to light or sound as quickly, making them much easier to catch. Remember that worms have the ability to regenerate an entire tail if necessary, so if you happen to tear a worm in half, you probably haven't killed it.

Several different types of worm are used across North America and the most common names given to the different species are the following:

• Nightcrawlers are brownish red in color and grow on average to be 6 inches (15 cm) long. The nightcrawler can be found on sidewalks and roads after heavy rains, especially after dark.

• Angleworms, or garden worms, are more pinkish red in color and smaller, averaging 3 inches (7.6 cm) in length.

• Leafworms are similar to nightcrawlers in color but average only 4 inches (10 cm) in length and can be recognized by their flattened tail.

• Grunt worms are collected by using noise and vibration to get them to the surface—there are several different types. They average 6 inches in length and their color may vary from pink to brown to gray.

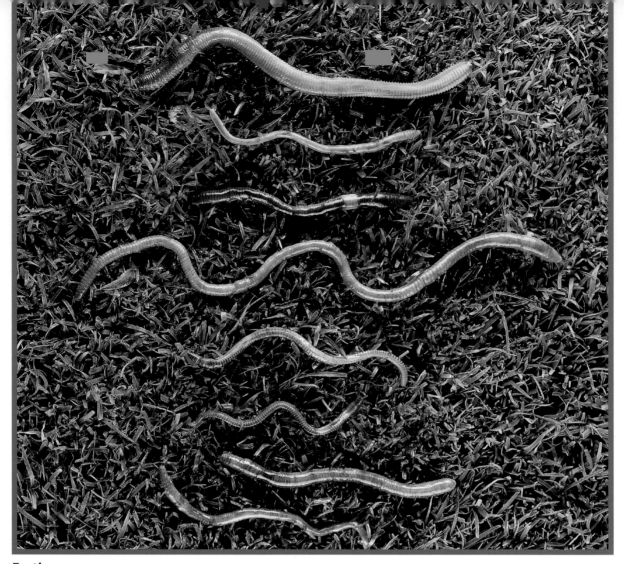

Earthworms work well for bait. From top to bottom are: nightcrawler (sometimes called dew or rain worm), garden worm (often called angleworm or fishworm), leaf worm, grunt worm, manure worm (also called red worm), red wiggler, gray nightcrawler, African nightcrawler.

• Manure worms are primarily raised commercially in the South and sold throughout North America as the red worm. They are red with whitish bands along the body, and average 3 inches (7.6 cm) in length. Another popular manure worm is the red wiggler, which averages 2 inches (5 cm) in length and is also commercially grown.

• Gray nightcrawlers are commercially grown in sand and peat. They quickly grow to an average length of 4 inches (10 cm). These pinkish gray worms thrash wildly when touched, making them a challenge to handle.

• African nightcrawlers are raised commercially in Africa. This species of worm is able to withstand warmer temperatures than other earthworms. Growing to 3 inches in length on average, their color is similar to that of the North American native nightcrawler.

Catching Worms

I started what ended up being my most profitable business venture by collecting worms at the age of twelve. The idea came from my need to generate money to attend Camp Fish. I caught and sold thousands of worms and crawlers and earned enough to pay my camp fees for the next summer.

Spring was the easiest time to collect worms for me because the soil was saturated from spring rains. Worms typically live only 2 or 3 feet (0.6 or 1 m) below the surface at this time of the year. During the summer months they can burrow up to 15 feet (4.5 m) deep if the soil becomes very dry.

Nightcrawlers and other worms breathe through their skin, so when heavy rains flood their burrows they must come to the surface to avoid drowning. This is the reason you see so many worms on your driveway or in the road after a heavy rain. After dark, nightcrawlers and worms come to the surface. The best-case scenario is when there is enough rain to drive them completely from their burrows. As mentioned earlier, if the ground is not saturated, night-crawlers leave their tail anchored in the burrow for security and may end up getting away.

My technique for catching worms when I was twelve still works today. I liked to gear up with a 1-gallon (3.8-l), plastic ice cream pail filled with potting soil or commercially sold worm bedding (shredded paper). Then I would quietly search my backyard. I found that a headlamp worked best because on many nights I need-ed both hands to be successful.

As my business grew, so did the need to harvest worms, even when it didn't rain for weeks. I supplied a large bait shop just a block away from our house and they needed worms at all times! A grade-school friend of mine solved the problem by showing me that if I ran a hose over the ground for several hours the worms would come to the sur-face. Many parks, golf courses and baseball fields also produce good numbers of worms if you do not have access to a produc-tive yard. Be sure to ask permis-sion if necessary.

When the need to expand my business came, I began search-ing the large compost pile next to our garage. Our compost pile consisted of grass clippings, leaves and spent annuals from the previous season of garden-ing. Here I found leaf worms, angleworms and some larger nightcrawlers.

Manure worms are harvested by scouting around barns, sta-bles and other areas with manure or decaying organic materials.

Anglers in the Southeast have success harvesting grunt worms in pine-studded forests because these worms prefer a more acidic soil. Hillsides are also good spots when condi-tions are wet; lowlands are best during the dry seasons.

Grab a nightcrawler firmly by the head. The worm has several rows of tiny bristles that enable it to grip the walls of its burrow (shown in cross section here). Exert steady pressure until the worm tires and loosens its grip.

Worm containers are made of fiberboard, Styrofoam or other porous material that allows oxygen to penetrate but keeps out water. They should have tight-fitting lids to keep the bedding moist and to prevent the worms from crawling out. Some anglers make their own worm boxes of wood and window screen. Containers used on fishing trips should be well insulated. Some have refreezable ice packs built into the cover.

Keeping Worms

You can, as I did, keep worms in Styrofoam worm boxes purchased at the bait store. A homemade fiberboard box or Styrofoam cooler also works, as long as the material is porous so the worms can breathe when the cover is on. The worm boxes I bought came with bedding made of shredded newspaper, which needed to be moistened with water before placing the worms in their new home. I experimented with other bedding and found that store-bought sphagnum moss worked the best for storing worms long term and was not as messy to deal with as potting soil.

I could keep sixty or so worms in a 24- by 12-inch (60- by 30-cm) worm box, provided I kept it well moistened and in the cooler temperatures of our basement. Checking the boxes every few days, to remove any dead worms and remoisten the bedding, allowed me to keep the worms healthy longer.

Although I fed my worms store-bought food, my secret to generating larger worms than my competition was to add a layer of water-soaked newspaper to the top of the bedding. The worms then absorbed the excess water from the newspaper and swelled to twice the size they were when harvested. You have to be careful not to drown them, however—this was a trial-and-error process in the beginning.

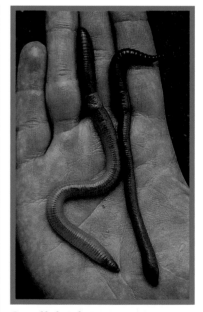

Conditioning makes crawlers larger and more vigorous. During conditioning, the crawler on the left absorbed water from the paper, swelling to nearly twice normal size.

Leeches

Most leeches feed on dead or decaying animal flesh. Just a few species feed only through the skin of animals; one of these is the horse leech. Many anglers confuse bloodsuckers and leeches; they think they're the same species. In fact, however, true bloodsuckers (like the medicine leech) have actual jaws and are able to tear through skin to reach blood vessels and tissue.

Many fish species enjoy a regular diet of leeches, but they often prefer certain species of leech. The most commonly used leech for bait is the ribbon leech. In some parts of the country anglers use the tiger leech for panfish because, when mature, it has a smaller profile and is very lively on a hook. The least productive members of the leech family are the horse and medicine leeches; they are both lifeless when put on a hook.

Catching and Keeping Leeches

Leeches are sold at most bait shops across the north-central U.S. and south-central Canada, but are rarely for sale in other parts of the country. If you fish in a part of the country where leeches are hard to come by, there's hope. Trapping them is not a difficult thing to do.

Once the water temperature reaches 50°F (10°C), leeches come out of their winter hibernation in search of food. When scouting for a good area to trap, keep in mind that the body of water should not have any significant numbers of gamefish.

Ribbon leeches squirm actively when held. A ribbon leech has a firm body and body striations and grooves that are not very pronounced. By contrast, a tiger leech is smaller, thinner and lighter in color with two to four rows of faint black spots extending down the back.

Medicine leeches and horse leeches (top to bottom) are not very effective as bait. Their bodies are soft and limp, both in the hand and on the hook. The medicine leach has a reddish orange belly and rows of red dots down the back.

Catch your leeches in a coffee-can trap (top) by placing the bait in the can, then crimping the top. Also effective is a gunny-sack trap (above) attached to ropes, and tossed into shallow water. The leeches squeeze through the fabric to reach the bait. Containers to keep leeches healthy while fishing (left) are also popular with anglers.

Fatheads and other small minnows in a body of water is a good sign to look for. After they spawn in late spring to early summer, many of the adult minnows die off, providing a food source that can support a large population of leeches. Small bodies of water surrounded by cattails and containing lily pads and algae usually support the largest populations of leeches.

Once you have located a body of water with a good likelihood of having a large population of leeches, there are two common ways to trap them: with a coffee-can trap or a gunnysack trap. No matter what method you choose, be sure to check, clean and re-bait your traps often. This will result in the best harvest for the time spent.

Keeping leeches is much easier than keeping most other live bait. They are able to withstand greater temperature changes than, say, minnows but soon become lifeless and die if left in direct sunlight or on the hook too long while fishing. If you follow these simple tips you'll be able to keep leeches caught in the spring, well into fall: Keep your leeches in a cool place, change the water often and discard any dead ones.

Even without food, leeches can last several months, shrinking only a little. To keep them at their best, toss in some of your dead minnows for the leeches to feed on. Many bait stores sell several types of containers know as "lockers" for leeches. Some anglers seem to prefer the plasic variety, but Styrofoam coolers and minnow buckets work well too.

Insects

Whether or not you call them "bugs" or consider them a nuisance to your fishing trip, insects are actually a very important food source for many fish species. In fact, without a good population of aquatic insects, waterways cannot support anything but minimal fish populations.

Having a basic knowledge of the life cycles of insects can be the difference in angling success and failure.

Aquatic Insects

Almost every body of water provides a freshwater habitat for some type of insect life. Aquatic insects spend the early stages of their lives in the water and move to the surface to become adults.

Below the water's surface, these immature insects are known as larvae. They are wingless and have tiny gills used for breathing. For many types of fish, insect larvae are a large part of their diet. Trout, panfish and young gamefish all rely heavily on insect larvae as a high-protein food source to help them grow quickly.

One group of aquatic insects, including mayflies, stoneflies, dragonflies and damselflies, are called nymphs when they are in their immature stage. Anglers who use nymphs as bait may not be aware of what species they hatch into as adults. Examples of common nymphs and their adult forms are the hellgrammite that hatches into a dobsonfly, a waterworm that becomes a cranefly and a hexagenia that is a species of mayfly in its adult form. These insects

crawl onto land, where they hatch into adults and fly away.

Insects feed and grow during this larval or nymphal stage. Depending on the species this period can last from two or three days to several years. As insects mature they begin to molt, which is the process of shedding the outer skin. Some species molt several times; others, only a few. The final molting session of an insect produces a winged, mature adult.

While it's true that fish eat immature insects at every stage of their transformation, they have the easiest access in the final stages. This is when huge numbers of insects have hatched in the water and make

Lift a rock, then check for nymphs or larvae on the underside. This is a good way to collect caddis cases, stonefly nymphs and other insect larvae.

The mayfly life cycle begins as eggs hatch into nymphs (1), which live in the streambed for up to two years. The emergence stage (2) begins as nymphs swim to the surface, where they emerge to become duns (3). Soon the duns fly to nearby vegetation and molt into spinners (4). After the adults mate over the water, the female deposits her eggs (5) and the adults die. The eggs sink to the streambed and the cycle begins anew.

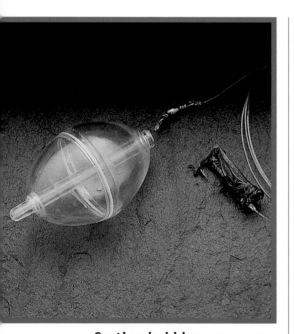

Casting bubbles add weight but will not spook fish. For extra casting distance, fill the bubble with water. When filled, the bubble sinks, carrying the bait to the fish in deep water.

their way to the surface to take flight.

Insects such as caddisflies and craneflies differ in their development: They hatch in the water and have a transitional period from their larval stage to adulthood. This is known as the pupa stage, when the insect lives in a cocoon-like case while becoming an adult.

The life span of adult aquatic insects is very short; it can last from just a few hours to several days, depending on the species. As an adult the insect's whole purpose in life is to lay eggs and propagate the species. The largest insect hatches take place during the warmest months of summer and occur early in the morning and in the evening. Large hatches often trigger fish into a feeding frenzy, that my fishing partners and I call "the crescendo."

Terrestrial Insects

The second type of insect that is used by anglers is a group referred as terrestrials. Basically, they spend their entire life on dry ground. The most popular species include crickets, grasshoppers and caterpillars. These species work best as bait during the heat of the summer, when their numbers are at their peak.

These terrestrials can be found lining the grassy shores of most bodies of water. Many species of fish move into the shallows to feed on these insects, which are loaded with much-needed nutrients. Periods of high winds and rain will blow or wash terrestrials into the water making them easy prey for waiting gamefish.

Other types of insect larvae that fish can't resist are waxworms, grubs and mealworms.

Catch aquatic insects by stirring up the bottom, then holding a fine mesh net downstream. You may have to kick aside rocks to dislodge insects underneath them. You can make your own collecting tool by replacing the middle tines of a pitchfork with metal screen.

Waxworms are found in old beehives that are sitting out of the sun and wind. Waxworms burrow into the small holes and channels to lay their eggs. Many anglers raise waxworm colonies to be sure they have a good supply of this popular live bait. Waxworms can be purchased from your local biological supply house. Most local bait stores also offer some types of waxworm. Keep them in sawdust at room temperature if you are planning to raise them.

Grubs are found in damp areas of soil and leaves or in the same areas as worms and crawlers. Typically smaller than worms or crawlers they can be equally as enticing as other popular live baits used for panfish and trout. They also should be kept in sawdust at room temperature.

Mealworms can be found in locations with damp, spoiled grain and grain products. They will hide in refuse, empty sacks and bins in these types of areas. Keep mealworms in the refrigerator in a plastic container with holes poked in the lid for ventilation. Fill the container with wheat bran or peat for bedding. For food, place a small piece of potato or carrot in the container with the worms. The piece of vegetable should be replaced every two days. Remember to remove any mold that may build up on the bedding. If not refrigerated, mealworms turn into black beetles and are of no use as a fishing bait.

Catching and Keeping Insects

Trout fishing is what really showed me the importance of knowing how and where to find insects. Because insects can be found near most bodies of water, they can be a real lifesaver if you should run low on bait or forget to bring it with you in the first place.

The first place I look is under medium to large rocks, then under any logs in or around the water's edge and, finally, I search the mud and grasses along the bank. When fishing moving water with a partner, a small seine can be used: Simply have one angler work the rocks and gravel with his or her feet dislodging any insects hiding on the bottom. The other angler is positioned farther downstream, just waiting to scoop up what comes by.

Grasshoppers and crickets can be caught using a butterfly net. Search grassy areas around bodies of water or in ditches along the roadside. Caterpillars can be caught by hand. Look for them on the leaves of trees and small bushes near lakes or wooded areas.

Keeping your harvest of aquatics can be done by storing them in a well-ventilated plastic container filled with damp leaves or in an aerated cooler. Crickets and grasshoppers can be stored in specially designed cricket cages that allow you to get them out without too many of them hopping away.

You can easily make a homemade container to keep your harvested terrestrials in. Use a plastic or Styrofoam container—soda bottles and small minnow buckets with several holes for ventilation work well. Fill the container with green leaves and grasses and keep it in a cool, dry place.

Salamanders and Frogs

Anglers in search of large gamefish insist that live salamanders and frogs are the bait of choice. Although not as readily available as many other types of live bait, they are very hardy and have great action when placed on a hook.

Salamanders

Because salamanders are more active in cooler temperatures, anglers tend to use them in the spring and, especially, in the fall. Salamanders, like other amphibians, absorb moisture through their skin, which must stay moist, so they are found in and around water and other damp areas.

There are more than 100 species of salamanders living in North America, with the south-eastern U.S. having the largest variety. Anglers often use the species that are most common in the area they are fishing. Of all the species that could be used for bait, the following are by far the most common:

- Mole salamanders (such as the tiger salamander) use their thick bodies to burrow into damp soil where they live and eat. They come out only after heavy rains or in the spring when they breed and lay their eggs in shallow ponds. As young larvae they live in water and develop into adults on land.

- Lungless salamanders, also known as spring lizards, can be found along the edges of cool springs, brooks or streams. Spring lizards are the best swimmers of the salamander family.

- Giant salamanders, including sirens, mudpuppies and waterdogs, live in water throughout their entire lives. They can be found in stagnant, shallow water with a soft bottom and prefer a lot of vegetation on the bottom to root around in for food.

Catching and Keeping Salamanders

Mole salamanders are the easiest to catch in the spring after the first rains of the year. Search for them near ponds and muddy, damp areas after dark. You can use a seine for harvesting in the larval stage, and your hands for adults.

Spring lizards can be found throughout the year under rotting leaves, logs and moss along edges of cool streams and brooks. Again, after a good rain and at night are the best times to search for them. Keep in mind that spring lizards move very fast, making them a challenge to catch.

Giant salamanders are either

seined or caught on hook and line in slow-moving canals or backwaters. To catch them on hook and line try an ultralight spinning outfit with a small bobber rig, small hook and a piece of worm for bait. (The same rig can be used to catch bullfrogs.) Try pinching down the barb on the hook to get the salamanders off quicker and to avoid injuring them.

All salamanders are very hardy creatures that do not require a lot of attention or food when storing them. Keep them in a cool place and periodically change their water or bedding (wet leaves and debris from the edge of a pond or creek). This allows you to keep your harvest for several weeks. You can feed them minnows and worms, although you should try to use them as soon as you can.

Frogs

Although the popularity of frogs as bait has declined greatly, many veteran anglers still consider frogs very effective bait for bass, catfish and northern pike. The decline of frog populations in many parts of the country is due to harvesting restrictions, disease, wetland drainage and pesticides, making frogs harder to come by than in the past.

As a member of the amphibian family, frogs have a larval stage, breathe through their skin and hibernate in the winter. The frog larval stage is called a tadpole, and although fish do eat tadpoles, they are much too delicate to put on a hook and use for bait.

Frogs burrow into muddy, bottom areas of lakes and deeper ponds in the fall, as the air temperature begins to cool. Knowing this may allow for one

Lift rocks or other objects that cover cool, damp soil to find mole salamanders. They move slowly and are easy to grab.

Shine a headlamp over rocks in a small stream to find spring lizards at night. Catching them with a long-handled dip net works well. Remember that approaching too quickly or too closely will scare them into the water and out of reach.

Popular frog species to use as bait for fishing are: leopard frogs (top left), bullfrogs (top right) and green frogs (lower left).

of the best fishing opportunities of the year.

I have friends who wait all year for the first hard frost of the fall to send the frogs to the nearest shallow, soft-bottom bay. Also at this time, largemouth bass often congregate in the shallow water, just waiting for a meal to swim off shore. You can cast lip-hooked frogs in the shallows and make some unbelievable catches.

Here are three popular frog species to try:

• Leopard frogs are the most common species of frogs used for bait, because they are found throughout most of North America. Reaching 4 inches (10 cm) in length, they have tell-tale brown spots and very distinctive ridges that run down the length of their back. They

are often found in damp, grassy meadows and grasses near the edges of water where they catch their insect meals.

• Green frogs are found throughout the eastern half of the United States and parts of southeastern Canada. Growing to 3 inches (7.6 cm) in length, they also have ridges that extend from the eye to about two-thirds of the way down their back. Typically, green frogs are found in marshlands or along small streams.

• Bullfrogs are the largest members of the North American frog family. This requires them to live near deeper water than most other frogs. Sometimes reaching 6 inches (15 cm) in length, bullfrogs are used as cut-bait by many anglers. Lakes,

bayous and deep ponds in the southeastern region of the United States are where the largest population of bullfrogs can be found.

Catching and Keeping Frogs

Harvesting frogs is best done in mid- to late summer after they have changed from tadpoles into adults. A few weeks after this transformation, frogs begin to migrate toward their winter areas. This phenomenon is known as the great frog migration to many anglers. You may see frogs by the thousands crossing a country road at night. Obviously, this is the best time to stock up for your next fishing trip.

Leopard and green frogs can be harvested by hand or with

nets, along marshes, creeks and small streams. Both of these frog species can also be seen along a road separating wetland areas, indicating the migration is in full swing.

Bullfrogs are caught typically at night with the use of headlamps. They seldom leave the aquatic vegetation near their watery homes so many anglers use nets and the hook-and-line method to catch them.

Frogs can present some challenges for anglers trying to keep them for extended periods of time. They are very susceptible to disease, and they can jump—high and long! Also, they require plenty of space, fresh water and several places to rest out of the water.

Frogs should be kept in a cool, well-ventilated container with a good lid to prevent escapes. Frogs eat insects like crickets or grasshoppers as well as worms. They should be fed about once every three weeks and used as soon as possible to be in their best condition.

Coolers can be used to store frogs, which need about an inch (2.5 cm) of water for good habitat. Add pieces of broken clay pots so the frogs have a place to climb out of the water. Change the water once each week. Discard frogs that appear unhealthy.

Catch a bullfrog or other large frog on a small, brightly colored yarn fly. Use a cane pole, light monofilament and a #10 hook. You can also net frogs from the bow of a boat poled through shoreline weedbeds. Shining a light in a frog's eyes makes it easier to approach and capture.

Crustaceans

Fish rely on crustaceans throughout their lives as a key element in their diet, especially when they are young. This fact makes them effective as live bait in many fishing situations.

Crustaceans have distinctive external skeletons or shells. As they grow they shed their shells in a process known as molting. Other features common to crustaceans are jointed legs and antennae and the fact that they typically breathe through gills. The members of the crustacean family that are used as food for freshwater fish species range in size from nearly microscopic to over 6 inches (15 cm) long.

Most anglers immediately think of crayfish as the crustacean that is most important to fish. But it is actually the smaller species of crustaceans that are eaten by young gamefish and panfish as they grow that are critical for fish populations in many lakes, streams, rivers and reservoirs. Important species include several types of freshwater shrimp and scuds.

The most common crustaceans used by freshwater anglers are the following.

• Crayfish are also known as crawfish, crawdads or crabs, depending on where you live. Found throughout North America, crayfish inhabit lakes, rivers, streams and sloughs. Crayfish can be found by looking around some type of cover on the bottom. They typically seek out rocks, wood or weeds in the water they inhabit.

• Grass shrimp are transparent crustaceans found primarily in the freshwaters of the southeastern states.

• Scuds are found in the cool, unpolluted waters of many trout streams across North America. Rooted vegetation provides the rich oxygen and cover needed for scuds to thrive. They are also a key element to many trout species and have for years been the template for many fly patterns.

• Freshwater shrimp live in lakes, channels and backwaters connected to large river systems. These shrimp range from the brackish water of these systems (where they spawn) to the first major obstruction or dam. In the South they are known and sold as river shrimp.

Catching Crustaceans

Harvesting crustaceans is most productive after dark, while they are on the move looking for food. Their extreme sensitivity to light makes it hard for anglers to catch large numbers of crustaceans by hand. This factor makes traps the most productive way to collect ample numbers.

Anglers who want to collect a few crayfish by hand should search shallow, rocky areas of the shoreline—simply turn over the rocks and grab the crayfish as it scoots across the bottom. I recommend this be done with two or more people or you could spend more time chasing them than fishing. A small butterfly-type net is very helpful, as a pinch by a good-sized crayfish claw can make you let out quite a scream.

Harvesting large numbers of crayfish requires using a trap, seine or umbrella net. Traps should be baited with fresh meat that is chopped up to give off more scent, and then set overnight in areas with numerous

Crayfish

Grass shrimp

Scud

Freshwater shrimp

Minnow traps catch crayfish in shallow, rocky areas. Expand the entrance slightly and bail with a punctured can of cat food. Always remove your catch of crayfish daily.

rocks and crevices. Some of the best areas include rocky shore-lines, along dams, bridges and railroad tracks. (Rocky shore-lines that are created by dumping in large qualities of small to mid-sized rocks are known as riprap.) Offshore rock piles that are found in 5 to 25 feet (1.5 to 7.5 m) of water and are protected from the wind can also produce good numbers of crayfish. Where the current is noticeable, key in on slack-water areas with rocks or weedy areas that crayfish use for cover (seines work well for this).

Look for grass shrimp in cleaner freshwater lakes, around dense mats of floating vegetation or submerged weeds like coontail, hydrilla, milfoil and eelgrass. Hand nets and seines with fine mesh work best for collecting them in numbers.

Scuds, like grass shrimp, also inhabit vegetation in clear, cool streams and spring-fed ponds. Sift through shallow vegetation with fine-mesh hand nets and seines. Many scuds are very small and require a keen eye and gentle hand to collect them.

In the spring freshwater shrimp migrate to the warmer water provided by power plants located along estuaries and large rivers. During the summer anglers use willow branches like a net in lakes and backwaters connected to these estuaries and large rivers.

Keeping Crustaceans

Crayfish, shrimp and scuds all prefer cool (around 50°F/10°C) and well-oxygenated conditions to survive for extended periods of time. Crayfish and shrimp can be packed in Styrofoam coolers with ice and plenty of damp weeds or moss. This helps to keep their shells soft, which is believed to make them more productive as bait. I prefer to use flow-through bait buckets when fishing with crayfish or scuds for bait. Adding the ice to crayfish or shrimp keeps the meat firm, which keeps them on a hook better. Grass shrimp can be kept in water but their bodies quickly become soft, should they die.

Crayfish are the most tolerant of warmer temperatures and can be kept at room temperature for extended periods of time. You can also keep them in a small bait box for the day while you are fishing, without having to worry about them, as you may do with shrimp or scuds.

Scuds should be kept in fresh, cool and well-aerated water. The insulation of a Styrofoam bucket and the aeration of an aquarium pump work well. Add ice as needed to keep the water temperature cool.

Keeping crustaceans is easy. Shrimp (far left) do well in a big cooler with ice and a thick layer of weeds in the bottom. Place crayfish (near left) among layers of wet newspapers. Scuds require cool, fresh water. Use an insulated container in warm weather (bottom left). Grass shrimp (bottom right) prefer dry newspaper covering the ice.

Other Natural Baits

For some species of fish, the most productive baits during certain times of the year are fresh, but not alive. The most popular of these are salmon eggs (spawn), preserved baits and cut-bait. I realize that these are technically not live baits, but they are rigged and fished in situations identical to those when you use live bait. In fact, they can be substituted for live bait in most circumstances.

Salmon Eggs

When fishing for salmon and steelhead, especially in tough conditions, salmon eggs can be the most productive way to catch them. I was raised in an era of catch-and-release fishing for these species after many years of the catch-and-kill strategy. Stocking reductions caused populations to decline and fish limits to be reduced. Because of this, the use of hand-collected salmon eggs has been dramatically reduced where I live. Don't get me wrong, I'm not above using fresh spawn when conditions are tough or mentoring a new-comer to the sport; it's just that store-bought salmon eggs are the standard in my area now. Although many artificial egg patterns are available in tackle stores, nothing works quite like the real thing.

A milky substance that is emitted from fresh salmon eggs flows through the current creating a sensory overload for salmon and steelhead, and oftentimes causes them to strike. You can hook a single egg, but spawn bags are the most popular way to fish with salmon eggs. The colored fine-mesh bags make them more durable when threaded on a hook, rather than handling the fragile eggs.

In areas where salmon and steelhead fishing is popular the local bait shops often have fresh spawn sacs for sale. Spawn bags can be in short supply during certain times of the year. If you're an avid do-it-yourselfer you can certainly make and keep your own.

How to Prepare Chunked Spawn

Wrap individual skeins in paper towels, well-drained and free of excess blood. Refrigerate for 2 to 3 days to remove remaining moisture.

Cut off ¾-inch (2-cm) square pieces, each with skein membrane attached. Drop egg chunks into powdered, non-detergent borax.

Roll the pieces in borax until coated. Borax preserves the eggs but washes off quickly when the bait is dropped into the water.

Drop chunks into a jar with a 1-inch (2.5-cm) layer of borax. Cover with airtight lid. Shake to coat again. Refrigerate in the jar for up to 2 weeks, or freeze.

Preserved Baits

When I worked at a sporting goods store in high school, I remember the first time a customer asked for ten dozen salted minnows for a trip to Canada. I was not prepared for this request, but over the years I came to learn that it was not an uncommon one. Anglers have used preserved bait for years when fishing in remote areas or where regulations didn't allow the use of live bait.

Nearly any live bait can be preserved in bottles with formaldehyde, freeze-dried quickly at extremely cold temperatures or cured using a salt-sugar method. Remember that before using freeze-dried baits, they need to be soaked in water. Bottled and salted baits, on the other hand, are ready to use in their lifelike state.

If you're not able to find a particular preserved bait at your local bait shop, you may find it offered on the Internet. Many manufacturers ship directly to anglers.

Although preserved baits typically do not out-produce live bait they still are a great alternative when you don't have access to live bait.

Cut-Bait and Fish Parts

Cut-bait is a cost-effective and oftentimes very successful bait for certain species of fish. White bass, yellow perch, rock bass, crappies, bullheads and channel catfish come to mind when I think of great candidates to chop up for cut-bait.

Oily fish, such as smelt, alewives, anchovies, shad and herring, give off the most scent when used as cut-bait. Suckers,

How to Cure Baitfish

Cure baitfish in a mixture of equal parts of salt and sugar. Keep them in ice cream buckets or other plastic or glass containers.

Form a single layer of fish on a ½-inch (12.7-mm) bed of the salt-sugar mixture. Make sure the fish do not touch each other or the salt will not penetrate.

Add several more layers of salt and baitfish. The bait will be preserved after 48 hours at room temperature. Refrigerate the fish in plastic bags.

carp, red horse and other rough fish can work equally well. As is true with live bait, cut-bait is often popular regionally, largely based on availability.

One of the most popular fish parts I use is for ice fishing. I use just the head of a fresh fathead minnow to tip my jigging spoon. I may catch several perch, walleye or catfish on a single head. I change the head often because the scent that is emitted from the severed head lasts no more than half an hour.

When fishing for cats I prefer to cut a medium-size sucker into chunks, thread a 1/0 hook through both sides of the bait and fish it on a bottom rig. The size of the chunk depends on the size of cats I plan to catch. Anytime I use cut-bait I use a sharp knife to make small slits in the bait chunk, which allows more fish-attracting fluids to escape.

In areas where lake trout are popular, anglers use strips of suckers and herring meat fished on the bottom or tipped on a jig. Another underrated technique for cut-bait is to use 3- or 4-inch (7.6- or 10-cm) sucker strips as a teaser on spoons or spinnerbaits for big northern pike. The added action and sucker smell can lead to ferocious strikes.

Grocery Store Angling

The grocery store is where many anglers, including myself, go to find some of the most commonly used bait. Here are three examples that have been used to catch fish for years:

• Marshmallows work great for floating an angleworm off the bottom when fishing trout.

• Whole-kernel corn threaded onto a long-shank hook can produce bites from bullheads, carp, catfish and panfish.

• Chicken liver can be drifted under a bobber or fished on the bottom for carp and catfish. Make small slits in the liver to increase the scent released into the water.

Chapter 3

Scents and Doughbaits

You see them advertised in nearly every fishing publication on the newsstand. You see them used on nearly every popular fishing show on television. No, I am not talking about some new fishing lure or a fancy fishing boat; I am talking about scents and doughbaits.

They are a special category of bait. They are obviously not live bait, but are also not an artificial lure. In various parts of the country, they're extremely popular.

Like live bait, scents and doughbaits work on a fish's sense of smell to convince a fish that the bait is real, or mask unnatural odors that may alarm a feeding fish.

Scents

Whether you believe in using fish scents or not, I can tell you this: You will find a bottle or can of scent tucked away in many an angler's gear bag, even if they won't admit it. I have found that scents tend to increase the amount of time a fish will hold onto bait, whether it's alive or dead.

Scent manufacturers have tried numerous different recipes to create the ultimate attractant using chopped-up fish parts, fish oils, synthetic oils or pheromones just to name a few. Unfortunately, a number of these companies have gone out of business; whether their product worked or not is still open for debate.

One fact is routinely accepted: Scents can cover up human,

gasoline or other unnatural smells that get on your bait from handling it or from coming in contact with the floor of the boat. The ability to get rid of these scents often leads to more catches.

Most fish scents are designed and sold to attract certain species of gamefish; other scents, such as garlic, anise oil and various baitfish, are marketed for any type of gamefish. Scent containers come in all shapes and sizes, making it easy for you to find one that fits perfectly in your tackle bag.

The most common forms of fish scent are available in liquid,

aerosol, paste and gel. I prefer aerosol and liquid scents because of the ease of application. But throughout the year I use every type, depending on the fish I'm after.

I try to find scents that contain chopped-up fish or crayfish parts and/or fish pheromones. Pheromones are the biological scents that animals give off. Those used in fish scents are believed to trigger feeding instincts in predators by mimicking the escape or fear pheromones released by baitfish.

I frequently apply scent to my bait throughout the day, and it's become a confidence booster for me.

Scents come in an astonishing array of options. No matter when or where you're fishing, or what you're fishing for, there is sure to be a product that will meet your needs.

Dip-baits come in a variety of scents and anglers can choose from special worm rigs or sponge hooks to hold their favorite dip.

Doughbaits and Dip-Baits

Obviously, doughbaits and dip-baits (pastes) are not live bait, but because of the way they are fished, stored and rigged on the hook, they are closer to live bait than artificial lures. They are nearly always fished on a plain hook, bottom rig or some type of bobber rig. They are also used in situations where the angler is already fishing with live bait on the same rig or has live bait on other rods for the same fish. And if you are a catfish angler, keep in mind that doughs and dips often out-fish live bait in many situations.

Doughbaits

Many secret doughbait recipes have been handed down for years, mostly by die-hard carp and catfish anglers. Doughbaits are typically some type of cornmeal or flour that is mixed with water, brought to a boil then kneaded to the right consistency. Other ingredients, such as Jell-O, peanut butter, black Karo syrup, sugar or vanilla, can be added for flavor. They can then be refrigerated until the next fishing trip and will last up to three weeks.

Pre-made doughbaits are often popular regionally and can be found in local bait shops where fishing for catfish and carp is popular. Many shops carry a large selection of commercially manufactured doughbaits that work great. The Internet is also a good place to search for doughbaits, as many manufacturers will ship products right to your door.

To fish with doughbait simply tear off a chunk of dough and form it around a #4 or #2 treble hook. The dough floats off the hook at the bottom, making it easy for hungry catfish and carp to find. When fishing moving water the doughbait may dissolve quicker, so don't be afraid to replace it often.

As the dough dissolves it leaves a scent trail in the water signaling the fish in the area. Doughbaits can also be fished under a slip-bobber when you're trying to cover more water.

Commercial doughbaits

come in plastic tubs. A variety of hook types can be effective; use whatever combination you find works best for you. Mold the doughbait into a firm ball around the hook.

Dip-Baits

Store-bought pastes, often called dip-baits, differ from doughbait in consistency. These have a sticky feel and anglers can spread them onto just about anything to give it a fish-attracting smell.

Dip-baits come in a variety of scents—garlic, cheese, blood, shad, shrimp and liver are the most popular. Some have several ingredients combined into one nasty-smelling dip. Anglers can choose from special worm rigs or sponge hooks to hold their favorite dip.

Dip-baits and pastes are mainly used for catching smaller, eating-size catfish. Like doughbaits, they are very effective when you're fishing moving water. The scent travels downstream and

Dip-baits also can be used on a "catfish worm." It's a short, thick plastic grub with rings or dimples to hold the dip-bait, with a snelled hook buried in the tail.

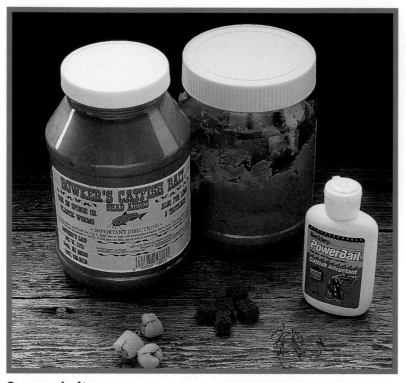

Sponge baits have a thinner consistency than dip-baits, so sponge-covered treble hooks are used to soak up the bait for fishing. Sponge baits are effective even in swift currents.

Tube baits are packaged in long, soft-plastic tubes. They are usually fished in specially made plastic lures or protein-based bladders that come in a variety of shapes and sizes.

attracts fish to the bait. Doughbaits and dip-baits are pretty much the same products, except that dip-baits are often softer and are too mushy to form into a ball.

I highly recommend using rubber gloves or a stick to apply dip-baits to your hook, as many of these smelly concoctions can linger for hours after coming in contact with your skin or clothes. Read the directions on the container for proper storage of a purchased dip.

If you make your own dip, you can keep it for about six months if you keep it refrigerated. Be sure to watch for mold developing—that's a sure sign you need to make a new batch.

Sponge Baits

Sponge baits, as the name suggests, are nothing more than a piece of absorbent sponge molded around a treble hook. The sponges themselves are designed of very porous and durable synthetic material that slowly emits dips and pastes that are either molded to the sponge or added to the sponge by the angler. This can be done with a stick or rubber gloves.

The sponge also helps float the bait off the bottom. This makes it easier for carp and catfish to find the bait, particularly when fishing silt-covered bottom areas, which are found in many areas these species inhabit.

Remember to set the hook like you mean it, because the treble hooks are slightly guarded by the sponge material and you need a strong set to get the hook into the fish's mouth.

Tube Baits

Tube baits are similar to

Sponge baits attract catfish. Soak the sponge in scent. Fish the sponge in one spot or drift it slowly along the bottom. Reapply scent every half hour or so. The sponge stays on the hook well and releases the scent slowly.

sponge baits in that they are used in conjunction with dips and pastes. The difference is that tubes are made with heavy-duty tubing threaded over the shank of the treble hook instead of a sponge material. This heavy-duty tubing has several scent-releasing holes throughout its length.

Tube baits allow for better hooking potential in many cases because the tubing does not fill the entire gap of the hook. Both sponge baits and tube baits can be found in several bright colors such as red, orange, pink and chartreuse.

Either sponge or tube baits used with dips and pastes are the best choice when fishing for eating-size channel and blue catfish. If you're after carp, that's another story because these styles of bait holders will attract all sizes of this wary fish.

I recommend fishing both tube and sponge baits on a split-shot or slip-sinker rig; these rigs with allow you to adjust your leader length depending on how high off the

Chunk baits are quick and easy to hook. They melt slowly, making them perfect for trotlining. A piece of chunk bait on every third hook attracts fish to other baits on a trotline.

bottom you need to float your bait. Feel free to experiment with different colors of baits and flavors of dips and pastes until you find the right combination. Once you have found what works best for you, make a note of it somewhere; you may want to refer back to it year after year.

Chunk Baits

These pre-packaged baits are dense chunks, often made with the same ingredients found in dips and pastes. This is by far the cleanest style of bait in this category. The dense consistency of chunk baits allows anglers to keep their line in the water longer because the baits have a slower dissolve time.

Chunk baits also help reduce the chance of small fish nibbling the hook clean before attracting a larger fish. You simply thread them onto a single or treble hook and begin fishing. A split-shot and slip-sinker are recommended for fishing them on the bottom,

but they can also be suspended under a bobber when you need to cover more water. If you are looking for quick and easy bait for catfish and carp, chunk baits are your best bet.

PowerBaits®

This product was introduced by fishing-industry-giant Berkley®, located in Spirit Lake, Iowa. It is a lab-created formula of fish-attracting scents that cause fish to bite by fooling their senses into thinking they have real food. PowerBaits can be purchased as pre-formed balls, chunks and pastes. In these forms it is primarily used to catch trout, catfish and carp. They are highly effective and can out-fish live bait in some instances.

PowerBait is also formed into small, pan-fish-size worms and other small baits that are sold for both summer and winter fishing. The formula is

also used to produce plastics for catching larger species.

Gulp® is the latest release from the labs at Berkley. This 100% all-natural and biodegradable bait releases scent into the water 400 times faster than other types of plastic-based scent-enhanced products. It's also 100% biodegradable and eliminates the worry of littering the bottom of the lake.

Many anglers consider these products a crossover between artificial bait and live bait. One thing is sure, PowerBaits do catch fish.

Homemade Doughbait, Dip-Bait & Chunk-Bait Recipes

Doughbait Recipe

1 cup (2.3 dl) purified water
1 tablespoon (15 ml) vanilla
1 package (3 ounces) cherry Jell-O
1 cup (140 g) flour
1 tablespoon (15 ml) sugar
2 cups (320 g) cornmeal

Bring the water, vanilla and Jell-O to a boil. Mix the flour, cornmeal and sugar in a separate bowl and then slowly add it to the boiling water.

Let simmer for about five minutes or until the consistency is to your liking.

Refrigerate in a plastic bag until your next fishing adventure.

Dip-Bait Recipe

Dead, mashed minnows or shad
1 plastic container with lid
Limburger cheese (optional)
Anise oil (optional)

Put the fish in the container—as much as you want for whatever size of batch you want to make. Bury it in the backyard for 3 or 4 days.

After you dig up the container, you can use it plain, or add shredded or melted Limburger cheese and a drop or two of anise oil.

A small sponge on a hook can be dipped in the mixture and will attract channel catfish.

Cheesy Doughbait

1 cup hamburger meat
1 cup Limburger cheese
2 tablespoons garlic
  powder
1/2 cup flour

Run hamburger through a food processor or blender to make a thick paste. Add cheese and garlic powder; knead thoroughly. Add enough flour to bring dough to the desired consistency.

Minnow or Shad Dip-Bait

Allow a mess of mashed minnows or shad to decay in a buried plastic freezer container. (Don't use a glass container as it could explode!) A small sponge on a hook saturated with this bait works well to attract channel catfish.

Trotline Chunk Bait

1 cup yellow cornmeal
1 cup flour
1/4 teaspoon anise oil
1 tin sardines, packed
  in oil

Mix all ingredients in a large bowl. Add small amounts of water to form a breadlike dough. Form dough into balls the size of a Ping-Pong ball and drop into boiling water for 3 minutes. Remove, drain on paper towels and allow to cool.

Chapter 4

Fish to Go After

"What are you catching?" is a commonly asked question at nearly every body of water you may visit. The problem is that in many instances anglers are not sure; they are catching whatever bites on the bait they have chosen. And that often leads to frustration and wasted time on the water.

But by knowing how various fish species behave and where they prefer to live, your bait will be a lot more effective. You'll have more fun—no matter what you're fishing for. And you'll find any of these gamefish to be delicious on the dinner table!

Panfish

In general, panfish is the name given to a group of fish that includes many species of sunfish—such as bluegills, pumpkinseeds, redears, greens—and two species of crappie—white and black—plus perch (which will be discussed separately).

These scrappy little battlers live in every kind of water, from 1-acre (.4-hectare) ponds to 1,000-acre (400-hectare) lakes, and most species can be caught throughout the year using the simplest equipment.

Studies show that anglers between the ages of five and six who have a good experience while fishing are more likely to continue the sport in later years. This makes fishing for panfish with live bait one of the best bets if you are a beginner or trying to get a youngster interested in the sport.

Where to Fish

Throughout the U.S. and southern Canada anglers are sure to find at least one species of panfish roaming in nearby waters. Catching panfish on live bait is typically very easy, giving anglers good practice and confidence to chase larger fish.

My father and godfather taught my brothers and me how to fish on a little lake in Wisconsin that was loaded with large crappies and sunfish. That is what really got me hooked on fishing. It seemed like every time we went we would catch lots of big panfish, and the action was non-stop. My godfather was also good about mixing in some fishing for larger fish like northern pike and largemouth bass. But when he could see that we were getting restless he would quickly get us back on the panfish, where the quick action was.

In many areas of the South anglers are able to fish panfish year-round. Northern anglers must wait for the ice to go out before the water warms to around 50°F (10°C) for open-water panfish action.

Panfish move to shallow areas seeking food. This time of year is your best opportunity for catching large numbers and bigger panfish.

Equipment

For panfish, I recommend using a #8 or #10 long-shank, thin-wire hook. Most panfish

Baits for sunfish include: (1) cricket, (2) grasshopper, (3) piece of nightcrawler, (4) garden worm, (5) red wiggler, (6) small leech, (7) minnow, (8) grass shrimp, (9) clam meat, (10) waxworm, (11) mealworm. Hook sizes range from a #10 with a cricket to a #6 with a garden worm. You can add natural bait to an artificial to make the lure more appealing. Sunfish will hold the lure an instant longer before spitting it out.

Use teardrop jigs in stained water tipped with your favorite live bait. Teardrops are offered in bright colors that create a more visible bait.

Use long-shanked hooks when fishing with live bait. Sunfish often take the bait deeply, and the long shank makes hook removal much easier.

have smaller mouths making the smaller gap of the hook easier for them to swallow. The thin wire allows the fish to hook itself, which is important when fishing with a beginner or when you may be enjoying the day and not paying close attention. The long shank makes it easier to thread on a juicy piece of nightcrawler or angleworm. And it helps unhook your catch if the fish should swallow the hook.

A 1-inch-diameter (2.5-cm), round, fixed bobber works great when fishing for shallow-water panfish. Set the bobber so the bait rides 8 to 10 inches (20 to 25 cm) above the bottom or over any structure. Remember to bring and use enough small split-shot so that

no more than half of the bobber is above the waterline. Place the small split-shot 8 to 10 inches above the hook.

Like many anglers, I started using a light-action spincast rod and reel combo with 6-pound-test (2.7-kg) line when I began my fishing career. I soon graduated to a light spinning outfit with 8-pound (3.6-kg) line once my hands were big enough to operate the bail properly. Spinning rods and reels are still my first choice when chasing panfish and I use 2- to 6-pound-test (0.9- to 2.7-kg) line, depending on the size of fish and structure they are holding in. Using a lighter line often gets more strikes when fishing for panfish.

A 1-inch (2.5-cm) piece of

For crappies, dangle the jig and minnow in front of the darker ones. During the spawning period, males turn blacker than females and strike more aggressively, so your chances of catching them are greater.

nightcrawler or angleworm threaded on a hook is still my number-one choice for sunfish. A small crappie minnow hooked behind the back dorsal fin is my choice for crappie, perch, rock bass and larger sunfish. I add a colored hook or teardrop when fishing water that is stained or muddied from heavy rains. Waxworms and other insect larvae are my second choice for panfish, especially when heavy fishing pressure is present. When using smaller insect larvae, be sure to just skin-hook them through the blunt end and don't be afraid to use up to three on one hook.

Spring

As the water warms to temperatures above 60°F (15°C),

crappies and sunfish begin to spawn in shallow, hard-bottom areas and on weedy flats. The fish tend to prefer shallow areas that have brush piles, large duck systems or dense emergent weed patches like lily pads, reeds and cattails.

During the spawning period, many of the same methods mentioned above work well for crappies and sunnies. Spawning areas for crappies are typically in 4 to 8 feet (1.2 to 2.4 m) of water. Crappies seek out hard-bottom areas with weeds but can be found regularly in less than 4 feet of water while spawning. Crappies often relate to some type of structure when spawning, such as weed beds, fallen trees, brush piles, reeds, cattails and bulrushes. These

Use several grubs hooked on the blunt end of a small teardrop jig or hook for sunfish.

For sunfish use a jig and piece of leech. The bait is small enough to catch nibblers, yet it will stay on the hook indefinitely.

are all good areas to check when the water warms to around 65°F (18°C).

A good bet is to fish a small crappie minnow rigged on a slip-bobber rig. Set the bait depth so it's 6 to 12 inches (15 to 30 cm) above spawning fish.

For sunfish, I prefer to switch to a small leech fished on a small slip-bobber rig with a small split-shot. Once you have located spawning sunfish anchor the boat a good distance from the spawning area and cast up to the fish. Spawning beds can be as shallow as 2 feet (60 cm), so be quiet and make a small splash with your slip-bobber and leech rig so as not to spook the fish. Be sure to hook the leech just below the sucker portion of its body. Use grasshoppers and crickets fished with a clear casting bobber for wary spawning sunfish.

Summer

During the summer months, panfish—particularly the larger ones—spend most of their time around deeper structure.

Sunfish can be found around weedy humps and along the edges of main-lake points, which are the largest open area of water in a given lake or reservoir. Most structure found out in the main lake is below the water surface where anglers often rely on electronics and maps to help narrow the search. Crappies seek out sunken brush piles, main-lake rock piles and sunken islands where they often suspend just above them.

Slowly troll or drift small jigs or spinners tipped with live bait to locate panfish. Schools of panfish appear as a grayish cloud on your locator. Once you find a school of fish, anchor and use a slip-bobber rig or fish a small jig and split-shot vertically over the side of the boat. Be sure to set your bobber so the bait rides 1 to 2 feet (30 to 60 cm) above the fish.

At this time of year, feeding habits of keeper-size panfish are unpredictable at best. If you find that the usual baits of crawlers or larvae are not producing, try a split-shot and plain hook tipped with a scud or grass shrimp. Both of these crustaceans are a main part of a sunfish's diet in the summer and may increase the number and size of fish you catch. Crappies can also be finicky eaters during the hot days of summer, so fish early morning and evening hours when the bite is the best.

The most productive method I use for deep, summer crappies is simply a plain hook and small split-shot #3/0 cast away from the boat over the school of fish. After you cast, feed slack out before engaging the reel. This allows the split-shot rig to fall slowly and naturally to the bottom. When the fish are biting well your split-shot rig shouldn't even hit the bottom before you have a fish. Crappies move around a lot while feeding so if the action slows, simply pull anchor and systematically reposition around the structure to stay with the school.

In mid- to late summer insect hatches reach their peak. It is at this time that crappies and sunfish are often reluctant to bite the usual fare of worms and minnows. In Minnesota, where I live, the mayfly and other insect hatches are very intense. Panfish gorge themselves for days making it very tough to catch a limit of bigger panfish because they are so tuned in to the hatching insect.

Fishing with mayflies, dragonflies, stoneflies and larvae-like waxworms often gives you the upper hand during the hatch. Go out in the late afternoon on calm nights and just wait for the hatch to begin. Watch for crappies and sunfish that are beginning to feed on these emerging insects. The top of the water looks as if someone is casting numerous small lures into the lake, leaving small rings that quickly disappear.

I recommend using the insect or larvae of your choice on a light, split-shot rig, #8 to #10 long-shank hook and a #3/0 split-shot. Slip-bobber rigs also work but many times the splash spooks feeding fish. Insect hatches may only last 45 minutes to 1 hour so make good use of your time and be prepared for the flurry.

Fall

I enjoy targeting larger panfish in the autumn, making their way back to shallow water to eat and fatten up for the winter. Look for fish gathered around channels, inlets and hard-bottom weed flats in 4 to 8 feet (1.2 to 2.4 m) of water. Cast these areas with slip-bobbers and 1/16-ounce (1.7-g) feather jigs tipped with waxworms, insect larvae or medium-size crappie minnows. Keep in mind that the fish are on the move during this time of year so stay in one area only if you are regularly catching keeper-size fish.

When fishing a split-shot rig over large schools of suspended panfish, the smaller fish are usually toward the top of the school. Try adding more split-shot to your rig to get down into the school to catch the larger fish.

Look for bodies of water that have large predator gamefish populations like bass, walleye and pike. Fluctuating water levels and sunken brush on or off the bank are good clues too. Many anglers downsize the line to 2- or 4-pound-test (0.9- to 1.8-kg) and use fluorocarbon in clear water.

Use a long cane pole or flyrod when fishing spawning panfish in clear water with heavy cover. Lift out the fish vertically.

Because perch are aggressive biters throughout most of the year, they are great fun for youngsters and anglers who enjoy a meal of fresh fish often. The largest populations of perch are found in large, sand-bottom lakes with little weed growth.

Spring

As the water warms to around 45°F (7°C) perch migrate to the shallows before spawning. Try fishing areas around docks, brush and sparsely weeded flats with sand-gravel bottoms. Use a bobber rig with a #4 or #6 long-shank hook tipped with a small leech or piece of crawler. I like to use a chartreuse or fluores-cent-orange hook. Perch are very easy to find and catch but you may have to sort through the little ones to get enough keep-ers for a good meal.

Once the water has warmed above 45°F (7°C) perch spawn in protected bays in depths of 5 to 12 feet (1.5 to 3.6 m). Look for areas with scattered weed clumps and brush featuring a sandy or gravel bottom. A slip-bobber rig tipped with a small leech or piece of crawler gets the job done at this time of year. Try using a 1/16-ounce (1.7-g) marabou jig, tipped with a leech to keep the smaller fish from consuming all of your bait.

After the spawn perch move just outside spawning areas and hold in 15 to 20 feet (4.5 to 6 m) of water for several weeks. Use an electric trolling motor or drift these depths with a slip-sinker or split-shot rig on the bottom to locate schools of post-spawn perch. A piece of crawler or small leech catches perch all year long; larger post-spawn perch can also be caught using small crappie minnows.

Perch

Perch weighing 1/2 to 3/4 pound (0.23 to 0.4 kg) are con-sidered eating size, although they can grow to well over 1 pound/28 g (known as jumbos). I recommend using a light-action spincast or spinning combo spooled with 4- to 6- pound (1.8- to 2.7-kg) mono-filament line. The lighter tackle increases the fun factor when catching these tasty fish.

Where to Fish

Found throughout the north-ern U.S. and most of Canada, perch are a cool-water fish pre-ferring water temperatures from about 65 to 73°F (18 to 23°C).

Summer

As the long, warm days of summer progress, perch slide to deeper, cooler water, many times suspending over open water. Through summer perch feed on plankton, mayfly larvae and baitfish near the bottom or suspended over open water. Perch seek the cooler water temperatures found in depths of 25 to 35 feet (7.6 to 10.5 m). They often use the same areas as walleyes, so be sure to also search rocky humps, reefs and main-lake points that offer a deep feeding.

Drift or troll slip-sinker rigs on the bottom to locate fish then slow down and work the school vertically with a slip-bobber or small jig tipped with a crappie minnow or leech. If the perch are striking the bait with a half-hearted attempt, leaving you with a cleaned hook, try a double-hook crawler rig or use just the head of a crappie minnow.

Early and late in the day perch move up to feed in shallower depths from 8 to 12 feet (2.4 to 3.6 m), depending on water clarity. If the action slows on your midday hot spot try moving into shallow water to stay with the school. When perch move to shallow water to feed they tend to be more scattered so use your trolling motor and electronics to stay with small concentrations of fish.

Late summer produces some of the best insect hatches of the year and perch are one of the first freshwater gamefish to the dinner table during these hatches. Don't be surprised if the action is slow during the day when large hatches are occurring. Perch, like many other fish, feed for a short period of time in late afternoon into evening, often gorging themselves and making them less active during the day.

Use waxworms, larvae and mayflies with a colored hook on a split-shot or slip-bobber rig to tempt bloated perch. When reeling in perch, pay attention to whether they regurgitate the insects they are feeding on. This will give you an important clue to the size of the insects they are feeding on in a given body of water. Adjust the size of the bait you are using accordingly. Don't worry about the color or species of the insects they are feeding on—I find that the size is the biggest factor when selecting the most productive live bait.

Large insect hatches are commonly over open water where the bottom content is made up of primarily mud or silt. Find areas adjacent to sand- and gravel-bottom haunts where you were catching perch, but fishing suddenly slowed. Perch feeding on insects over soft-bottomed areas can be found throughout the water column; typically the largest fish in a school is within 5 to 10 feet (1.5 to 3 m) of the bottom. Soft-bottom areas should be fished with a slip-sinker rig tipped with a brightly colored spinner or small floating jig head to keep the piece of crawler, leech or crappie minnow off the bottom. The best methods are to drift and troll to find schools. Once located you can slow down and vertically fish over the school with slip-bobber rigs and small jigs.

When fishing small jigs for perch use a 1/16- to 1/8-ounce (1.7- to 3.5-g) version that has a #4 or #6 hook. Add split-shot to the line 18 inches (45 cm) above the jig to get a lighter jig down to the fish quickly. The deeper the water and the windier the day, the larger the split you should use. In general, bags of BB, 3/0 and #7 split-shot will cover most situations.

Fall

When the water in the shallows begins to cool in the fall perch in many lakes and reservoirs migrate onto shallower gravel and rocky flats or reefs to feed on baitfish. Riprap shorelines with scattered weed clumps also hold good numbers of perch fattening up for the long winter months ahead.

If the body of water you are fishing has any small tributaries or feeder creeks this would be a good place to start looking for concentrations of fish. Use slip-bobbers and small marabou jigs tipped with a crappie minnow or leech to tempt fall perch.

Use a thin strip of belly meat from a perch or a minnow head when perch are striking short. Either one provides necessary scent and your hooking percentage will be much higher.

Walleye

Here in my home state of Minnesota, the walleye is king. And for live-bait anglers, there is no better fish to be passionate about catching.

It is not surprising that the walleye is held in such high regard throughout North America. Its finicky feeding habits can frustrate even the most patient, expert anglers, so there is a feeling of accomplishment when a successful pattern is found, resulting in a good catch. Another reason for the walleye's popularity is its well-deserved reputation as table fare—it is simply one of the best-eating freshwater fish.

Where to Fish

Walleyes and saugers (a close relative) are found throughout the U.S. and most of Canada. Both have light-sensitive eyes and are known for their night-feeding prowess. A sauger's eye is even more light sensitive than a walleye's. This is why, even though these fish are very similar, saugers typically are caught in deeper water than walleyes; saugers also spawn deeper.

These great fish are found in lakes, reservoirs and rivers. In some cases they share the same water, which works out well because they don't have to compete for spawning areas or other seasonal holding spots due to their difference in depth preference.

Spring

When the water warms to 40°F (4°C)—typically March in the South and May in the North—walleyes and saugers move to structure in 15 to 30 feet (4.5 to 9 m) of water. This is the pre-spawn period and the fishing can be some of the best of the year for number and size of fish. Both fish spend several weeks at this depth, depending on weather and water clarity.

During the pre-spawn period a 6- to 7-foot (1.8- to 2.1-m) light-power spinning combo with 4- to 6-pound-test (1.8- to 2.7-kg) monofilament or fluorocarbon covers most situations. Anglers who encounter murky water on rivers may be able to

My Maiden Catch

I caught my first walleye when I was eleven; it was the third night of fishing at summer fishing camp. I had spent all day in the classroom taking notes while listening to several seminars on walleye fishing. I had not really digested all of the information the counselors had given us but I was excited to get out on the water.

Our guide was one of the most respected counselors at the camp, which made me more confident that I would catch my first walleye. They had warned us that not many walleyes lived in that lake but the fish that were caught were usually big.

Well, only two fish were caught that night and I caught one of them! It was a 27 1/2-inch, 7 1/4-pound (69.8-cm, 3.3-kg) walleye that had the whole camp talking.

We had been back-trolling with 1/4-ounce (7-g) jigs tipped with redtail chubs in 17 feet (5 m) of water off a sunken island when the big fish bit, just as the sun had set. The battle was epic but, lucky for me, one of the seminars that day had been on how to properly back-reel a fish instead of using your drag system.

Unfortunately, I must have fallen asleep during the important parts of this lesson because shortly after I started my battle with the fish I had something resembling a Jacob's ladder coming out of my spinning reel.

Happily, the fish was landed in spite of my fumbling.

---

get away with heavier line and a medium-power rod to help get their bait free from snags.

During stable weather walleyes and saugers bite pretty well during low-light periods. However, with these fish more than any other species, the first sign of unstable weather has them in a negative mood and very tough to catch. Vertical jigging accounts for most of the walleyes caught during this time of year.

Look for hard-bottom points, humps and reefs close to spawning areas. Reservoir anglers should look for fish in the deep water nearest major creek arms. Below the dam fish eddies and the first large pools you see. You should also check out the tailrace, which is the area below a dam where the cold water flows out from the reservoir.

Use a 1/8-ounce (3.5-g) jig tipped with a fathead, shiner or chub. This time of year, you can position the boat over the fish and drop the jig directly down to them, as they typically relate to the bottom. In murky water use a glow or chartreuse jig tipped with a big minnow.

Because the bites of walleyes are often subtle, start by using a stinger hook on your jig instead of missing a few fish and then adding one. During this time of year fish are tightly schooled and a couple of lost fish may slow the bite. It may also shut the school down completely, which is what many anglers experience when they are fishing large schools that are biting very aggressively. In the excitement, anglers oftentimes forget to check their line and hook point. This may result in a lost fish or two. Sometimes these fish swim back to the school and are believed to give off pheromones that alert other fish in the school of danger and cause the fish to stop biting altogether.

An electric trolling motor and a good fish locator are must-haves to effectively keep the boat over the fish. I like to use a flasher-style locator once I have found a group of fish on the graph.

Use a jig tipped with a fresh minnow to catch finicky walleyes. The action of the minnow is often all that is needed.

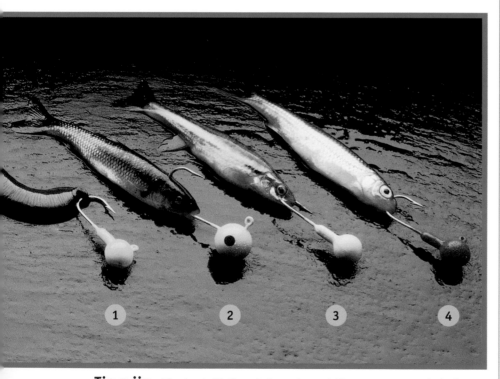

Tip a jig with a leech (1) through the sucker end. The most secure method of attaching a minnow is to (2) insert the hook point into the mouth and then push it out the top of the head. Other ways to hook a minnow are (3) hook it through the eye sockets or (4) push the hook through the lips, from the bottom up.

Pre-Spawn

Walleyes and saugers move into the shallows for a short period of time to fill up on food just before they spawn. Look for rocky shorelines with wind blowing into them, shallow humps and reefs or large, hard-bottom flats. Many of these fish tend to be found in water less than 8 feet (2.4 m) deep.

Reservoir anglers should search the upper ends of old creek channels and riprap banks with wind blowing into them. On rivers and reservoirs the fish migrate up-current and often congregate below dams. I still prefer a 1/8-ounce (3.5-mm) jig tipped with a minnow at this time of year but go down to 3/32 ounce (2.4 g) when the wind and current allow. You may have to go up to 3/4 ounce (20 g) in heavy winds or current. In this situation you are mainly casting the jig to fish that are feeding pretty well, so take off the stinger to minimize snags.

Should you encounter walleyes in water less than 3 feet (1 m) deep, and the water is clear, try a 3/0 split-shot and plain or colored #6 hook with a minnow. Another presentation I like to use is an in-line spinner, cast to the shallows and tipped with a minnow.

I also like to use spinners when fishing darker-colored rivers or in very windy conditions. The weight of the spinner depends on whether you elect to use a trolling motor or anchor the boat. Walleyes and saugers may school up in the shallows during this period but they will be on the move, so be prepared to keep watching for fish or go looking for them if they suddenly stop biting.

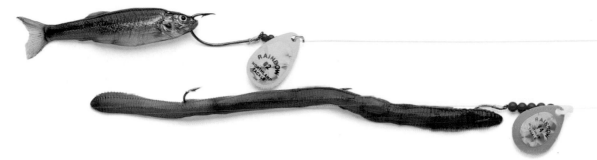

Live bait rigs with spinners attached can be used to trigger strikes from fish that are in a neutral feeding mood due to the rigors of spawning.

When walleyes and saugers begin to spawn the bite rate slows considerably. But because not all walleyes and saugers spawn at the same time, you can always find a biter somewhere in the system you are fishing. Start fishing stained-water lakes early and move to clear lakes as the weather warms up. This allows you to stay ahead of the spawn and keep your fishing more consistent. In reservoirs and rivers, you may not have to leave the body of water you're fishing, just the specific location.

Post-Spawn

After the spawn use a medium-power spinning combo that is 6 to 7 feet (1.8 to 2.1 m) in length and spooled with 6- to 8-pound-test (2.7- to 3.6-kg) monofilament for jigging and slip-bobber fishing. A 6½- to 8-foot (2- to 2.4-m) medium to medium-heavy baitcasting combo with 8- to 10-pound (3.6- to 4.5-kg) mono or super-line works best for pulling spinner rigs or heavy three-way rigs. I like to use rod holders when fishing multiple lines or when fishing with other anglers in a boat.

About two weeks after the spawn the bite picks up again; this is known as the post-spawn

period. Walleyes and saugers move to slow-tapering points and large gravel flats near spawning areas in lakes, often to the same locations where you found them during pre-spawn.

In reservoirs they move to flats and secondary points with a sloping break, along with the main creek channels. In rivers, post-spawn walleyes and saugers move to large rock or gravel points, deep holes and eddies just below spawning areas. The fish will be spread out and start feeding early and late in the day, but windy or overcast weather can have them biting all day.

A jig and minnow always catch fish, but post-spawn fish can be finicky, so covering water is the key to finding small groups of active fish. A three-way rig or bottom-bouncer is a good choice when trying to cover water searching for active fish. Use a ¾- to 1-ounce (20- to 28-g) sinker, depending on depth and current.

I like to start looking for fish in the 15- to 25-feet (4.5- to 7.5-m) range. The use of a small kicker motor is very helpful if the wind is whipping. Use a 3- or 4-foot (1- or 1.2-m) leader from the sinker with a #6 hook; if you need to use a spinner due to murky water,

stick to a #2 hook to keep your bait away from the spinner. Tip the hook with a nightcrawler, leech or minnow. (When using a nightcrawler I like to use a crawler harness, which consists of three hooks spaced 1½ inches/3.8 cm apart.) When you feel a bite, feed the fish a complete rod length of line before setting the hook; this gives the fish time to eat the bait. If hooking fish is a problem on any given day switch to a slip-sinker rig or let the fish take the bait longer.

Another good thing to do while trolling is to keep the bail open and your finger on the line. After a bite is detected let the line slip from your finger; begin counting to experiment with how long you need to wait before setting the hook. Active walleyes and saugers have a tendency to swallow the hook and bait completely, making catch-and-release difficult. If you experience this situation, you counted too long. To release deeply hooked fish, simply cut the line and tie on a new hook. This is why anglers use circle hooks: They avoid deeply hooking fish and you don't need to set the hook; you simply start reeling.

If fishing regulations allow it, return to these same areas in

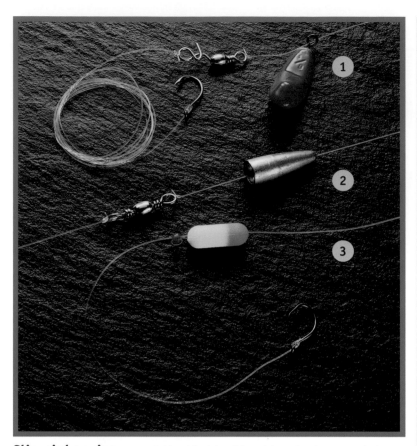

Slip-sinker rigs are available with: (1) walking sinkers, for clean or rocky bottoms; or (2) bullet sinkers, for weedy bottoms. Rigs with a float ahead of the hook (3) lift your bait above a blanket of weeds or reach fish holding a little off the bottom.

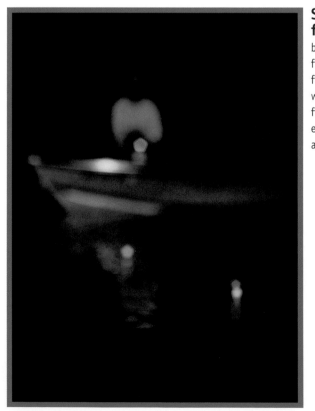

Slip-bobber fishing works better than using a fixed bobber for fishing in deep water. For night fishing, use a lighted float powered by a lithium battery.

the evening and try slip-bobber fishing for them. Several styles of lighted bobbers are available for anglers who like to fish at night. Even the finickiest of walleyes and saugers think about eating a leech or crawler dangling below a bobber.

Similar to the counting method I mentioned for slip-sinker rigs, try counting after the bobber goes down and again experiment with different lengths of time before setting the hook. Another thing to remember is to reel up all the slack in your line and wait until you feel the weight of the fish before setting the hook.

If your bobber comes back up to the surface while you are still counting, let it sit for a minute then bring it in and examine the bait to see how far in its mouth the fish had the bait. If the bite marks are only on the tail or halfway up the bait, try adding split-shot to the bobber. The fish may have felt too much resistance and let the bait go. Walleyes and saugers are very sensitive to resistance after they have picked up bait.

Summer

In the summer and fall periods, walleyes and saugers set up in open-water haunts and begin schooling. When the bite is on, several fish can be caught from a single school. In lakes look for main-lake points that plateau in 20 to 25 feet (6 to 7.5 m) of water. Also look for sand, gravel or rock humps in the same depths.

Reservoir anglers should check wooded humps and flats near the main creek channel or rocky main-lake points with a plateau for feeding. In rivers, I key on deep riprap banks with slight current, wing dams and the top end of deep pools.

Start fishing with 1- to 2-ounce (28- to 56-g) three-way rigs or bottom-bouncers, depending on wind, depth and current speed. You want to use enough weight so the line is almost vertical and still ticking the bottom, as you move along at speeds of 1.4 mph to 2.3 mph (2 to 3.7 kmph). Experiment with speed until the fish tell you what they want.

Summer is also the time to step up your spinner use. I prefer #2 and #4 Colorado blades. In stained or murky water I use bright colors like glow, fluorescent orange and green or chartreuse. Clear water calls for silver, gold, copper or black. Most of the

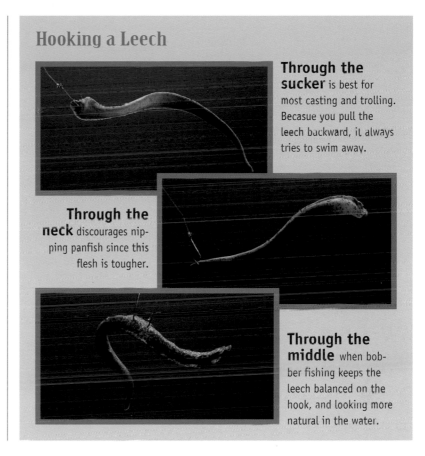

Hooking a Leech

Through the sucker is best for most casting and trolling. Becasue you pull the leech backward, it always tries to swim away.

Through the neck discourages nipping panfish since this flesh is tougher.

Through the middle when bobber fishing keeps the leech balanced on the hook, and looking more natural in the water.

Sweet-Spot Fishing

Once the water starts to cool in late summer, anglers slow down and use slip-sinker rigs and slip-bobber rigs to fish what are called "sweet spots" in an area. What does this mean? Simply, on every piece of structure there is something a little different that attracts fish in the largest numbers. Most of the time it is some type of change from what the rest of the piece of structure has to offer. It can be a transition in the bottom content from soft to hard, a small depression or a small rock pile on a sand flat. The key is to look for something different—the sweet spot. It usually has to do with the hardness of the bottom.

The beauty of understanding this strategy is that you can go to any lake, river or reservoir, pull up on a piece of structure and easily hit the sweet spot—if you know what to look for. And if the fish are not there, continue on and try a different type of structure but always look for its sweet spot. Continue the process until you pattern the fish on that day.

Your strategy should be to slow down and fish the structure you have located: Drift, using the trolling motor to make sure you get several good passes over the sweet spot with a slip-sinker rig tipped with a leech or crawler. A drift sock helps you adjust the boat speed to the fish's liking. Also, if you turn on all of the locators in your boat while drifting it may kick the fish out from under the boat even if they are down 20 feet (6 m). This is good because in many cases that is where your bait is. (If you have done some walleye fishing and experienced times when the angler in the back of the boat catches all the fish it may be due to the fact that all of the transducers are located back there.)

Suspended schools of fish that are marked on the depth finder should be noted and fished with a slip-bobber in late afternoon and into the evening.

Making and Using Breakaway Sinker Rigs

Cut a slit in the eye of a walking sinker (inset), then close the gap with a pair of pliers. If the sinker snags, a strong pull will open the eye and free the line, and you'll only lose the sinker.

For a mono dropper, tie a barrel swivel on one end of the dropper and pinch split-shot on the other. If the split-shot snag, give a strong tug to slide them off the dropper, then pinch on new ones.

time, I like to use a hammered blade over a flat finish, as it provides more flash.

You often have a small window of time for this summer pattern to be effective. Depending on weather and water temperatures you may only have 2 or 3 weeks of good, peak-summer fishing, so make good use of your time.

Armed with a GPS unit you can fish all of the likely areas where walleyes and saugers may hold. Keep track of where you contact fish. Chances are they use these bigger pieces of structure all year, but where exactly they hold on the structure often varies from year to year. So you may need to look a bit to find the exact spots they are using each year.

Fall

Autumn can bring some of the best action of the year. Walleyes and saugers are still active early and late in the day, but stable weather prolongs the bite. Overcast and windy days also extend the activity period. It's a good time to experiment with bait again—minnows, along with leeches and crawlers.

From late fall into winter or ice-up, anglers find walleyes and saugers bulking up before they become inactive as water temperatures drop below 40°F (4°C). This is the time to vertically fish a jig and minnow or slip-bobber tipped with a large fathead, shiner, redtail chub or sucker.

In lakes, fish the edge of bulrush patches on main-lake points (cast a jig and minnow up to the edge) and sharp breaks along reefs. In reservoirs, fish steep breaks along the main creek channel riddled with timber and inside turns along the old creek channel. In rivers, deep holes along the

outside bends and slow-moving slots in tailrace areas are key spots.

Walleyes and saugers can also be fished from the bank with live bait with good success. You just have to time it right—the period just before spawn and again in the fall when walleyes and saugers move into the shallows to bulk up before winter. Concentrate on areas where tributaries flow in or out, channels or neck downs (channels created by points of land that separate sections of a lake), and rocky or riprap banks close to deep water. Try a slip-sinker rig or lighted slip-bobber rigged with a large fathead, shiner, redtail chub or sucker in the 4- to 6-inch (10- to 15-cm) range. Fish early morning and late afternoon into the night, as this is the best time of year to catch some of the largest fish in those waters.

Northern Pike and Muskie

Living in the northern reaches of the United States, I have spent a fair share of my time chasing northern pike and muskies. The popularity and range of these two fish species have grown by leaps and bounds in recent years. To many anglers, catching a 25-pound (11-kg) pike or a 50-inch (127-cm) muskie would be the highlight of their fishing experience.

Where to Fish

Found throughout much of the northern portions of the U.S. and in Canada, these top predators really go for a good live-bait meal. Northern pike are typically very aggressive feeders, which makes them easy to catch throughout the year during daylight hours. Muskies, on the other hand, have a little more of an "attitude," which makes them more selective in their feeding habits.

I have caught pike with just about every type of lure or live bait. On the other hand, catching muskies on live bait takes a more precise approach and much more patience.

Equipment

To fish for northern pike and muskies you need the right equipment. A 6½-foot (2-m) medium-heavy to heavy-power rod with a spinning or baitcasting reel loaded with at least 17-pound-test (7.6-kg) line is a must. This rod and reel combination allows you to fish slip-bobber rigs with a 6- to 8-inch (15- to 20-cm) sucker minnow and slip-sinker rigs up to ¾ ounce (20 g) with a 6- to 8-inch (15- to 20-cm) sucker.

When fishing for trophy pike and muskies you should have a 6½- to 7½-foot (2- to 2.3-m) heavy-power rod and a good spinning or baitcasting reel. Braided Dacron and superlines are my favorites when I'm after the big ones. Even with Dacron and superlines I strongly recommend using a good-quality steel leader. Sure, many anglers have caught large pike and muskies on lighter tackle but the fight can last up to 20 minutes, which puts great stress on the fish if they are released. Many anglers do practice catch-and-release with trophy musky and pike, and a quick fight increases the chance of survival after release.

The hooks, sinkers and bobbers I use for pike and muskies are the largest in my tackle bag. Not only are their mouths bigger, but the largest members of these species will often eat minnows that are 10 inches (25 cm) or more in length. A good selection of hooks ranging from #1 to 4/0 in both live styles and treble hooks will get you started. Egg-sinkers and bottom-bouncers should range from 1/2 to 1 1/2 ounces (14 to 42 g), depending on the depth and size of bait you choose to use.

I call pike and muskie bobbers "buoys" because some anglers use sucker minnows up to 2 pounds (0.9 kg), which takes a very large bobber to keep it in the fish zone. A selection of 4- to 8-inch (10- to 20-cm) cylinder bobbers will get you started; the larger the bait the larger the bobber.

A good mouth spreader and a pair of long-nosed pliers are always with me when I head out on a pike and muskie trip. You have to remember that these fish have large, razor-sharp teeth and should be handled with caution.

Spring

In the spring, look for pike and muskies on shallow weed flats where they feed on minnows and panfish. Search flats using a 3/8- to 3/4-ounce (10.6- to 20-g) bucktail jig tipped with a 3- to 4-inch (7.6- to 10-cm) sucker or chub minnow. Once you have located a fish, slow down with a slip-bobber rig with the same sucker or chub minnow. I like to fish a slip-bobber rig set just above any new weed growth I can locate. Rather than casting these big minnows and risk

Hook Size and Baitfish Size

BAITFISH SIZE	HOOK STYLE & SIZE		
	Single	Treble	Quick-strike
4-5"	1/0, 2/0	4, 2	8
6-7"	2/0, 4/0	2, 1	6, 4
8-11"	4/0, 7/0	1, 1/0	4, 2
12-15"	7/0, 10/0	1/0, 3/0	2, 1/0

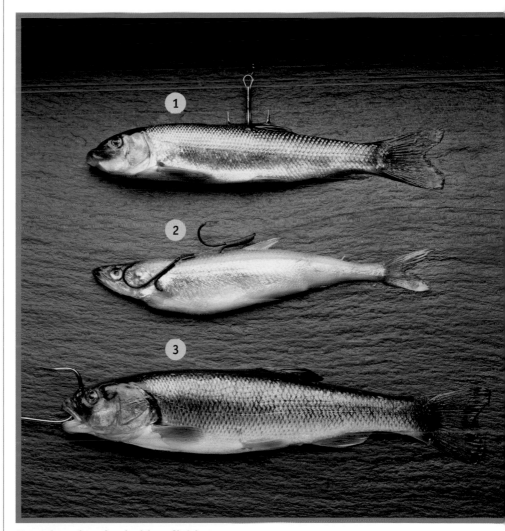

Popular rigs for bobber fishing with live or dead baitfish include: (1) treble hook with one prong pushed through the back; and (2) quick-strike rig, with the leading quick-strike hook just ahead of the dorsal fin and the trailing hook near the pectoral fin. Another excellent rig for live baitfish is (3) a single hook pushed through the snout only. This rig is tied with a Sneck hook, which has a squared-off bend, so more of the hook point stays exposed.

Floats include: (1) slot-, (2) cylinder- and (3) tube-style slip-bobbers, for working deep water; (4) clip-on and (5) peg bobbers, for fishing shallower water; and (6) a pop-off bobber, rigged to detach from the line when a fish strikes (inset).

killing my bait, I set the slip-bobber rig in the water and feed line out as the boat moves forward with the trolling motor until it is about 10 to 15 feet (3 to 4.5 m) back.

In states that allow two rods you can then continue to cast shallows with a jig and minnow. Larger pike and muskies often follow a jig and minnow to the boat—but don't eat. This is where having the slip-bobber rig can pay off. With this rig slowly moving along behind the boat, wary fish can take all the time they need before deciding to eat the minnow without the boat spooking them.

Remember to use a steel leader on all rigs and jigs. The sharp teeth that are found in both these fish's mouths would slice right through 20-pound (9-kg) monofilament lines.

Summer

During the summer months, pike and muskies can be found on deep weedlines, main-lake humps, points, rock piles and large weedbeds. I try to key in on locations that have a good, hard bottom. Sand and gravel areas have pike; I prefer a rocky bottom with weeds when I am focused on muskies.

Cast a 1/2- to 3/4-ounce (14- to 20-g) weedless-bucktail or silicone-skirted jig tipped with a 5- to 6-inch (13- to 15-cm) sucker minnow or chub along the weedline. Let the jig hit the bottom and fish it back to the boat by hopping it off the bottom, simulating a wounded baitfish. A 3/4-ounce (20-g) bottom-bouncer rig with a #1 or 1/0 hook tipped with a sucker or chub can be slowly trolled or drifted on the same weed edges to cover water while searching for fish.

Rivers also can have good numbers of pike and muskies. In fact, my largest muskie, a 52-incher (132-cm), was caught on the Mississippi River north of Minneapolis, Minnesota. Pike and muskies can be found in slow-moving flats, deeper holes protected from the main current and in backwater sloughs. Casting a 1/2- to 3/4-ounce (14-

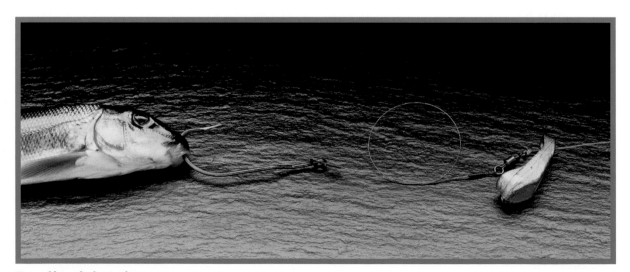

For slip-sinker rigs, slide a slip-sinker onto your line. Then, add a 3-foot (1-m) braided-wire leader. Push a single hook or floating jighead through the baitfish's snout. This rig, also used for casting, trolling and drifting, allows a fish to take line without feeling resistance.

Jerking live bait is an unusual but effective method for big pike and muskies. It combines the action of a jerkbait with the appeal of live bait. When you see or feel a strike, wait until you think the fish has swallowed the bait before setting the hook.

to 20-g) jig tipped with a 5- to 6-inch (13- to 15-cm) sucker or chub is how I fish these deeper holes and flats. The same method works for backwater sloughs but I use a 3/8-ounce (10.6-g) jig and minnow, and swim the bait over the top and through any weed growth. A 1/2-ounce spinner bait tipped with a 3- to 4-inch (7.6- to 10-cm) sucker or chub allows you to cover water quickly and get through the weeds that are often found in backwater areas.

Pike are most active during the daytime whereas muskies bite well after dark.

Fall

Autumn is a great time to chase larger pike and muskies. You can search main-lake points and turns along the shore using a bottom-bouncer rig tipped with a 6- to 10-inch (15- to 25-cm) sucker, chub, waterdog or salamander. Let out enough line so the weight just ticks the bottom and use a trolling motor or small outboard to work the edges of these structures. Pay attention to small changes in the bottom content and contour; these areas often hold fish.

Anchoring and slip-bobber fishing these same areas is also a very productive method of catching these coldwater predators. I prefer to use two anchors, one in the front and the other in the back, so the boat does not spin and tangle

Using quick-strike rigs makes the successful release of large pike or muskie easy. As the name suggests, this rig allows you to set the hook right away so the fish cannot swallow it.

my lines. A 10-inch (25-cm) sucker is no fun to cast and will be less lively if it is cast long distances repeatedly. If you do have to cast, a gentle lob works best. If you can, simply lower the minnow and bobber into the water off the end of the rod and feed slack to the bobber as the sucker begins to float away.

Keep the bobber in close range—about 15 or 20 feet (4.5 or 6 m) off the side of the boat. When a pike or muskie pulls the bobber down, feed it line for a minute or two. The time you wait until you set the hook

depends on how big your bait is; the larger the bait the longer you wait. Then reel up the slack and set the hook firmly, keeping pressure on the fish until you land it.

When I fish waters with large pike and muskies I like to pull the anchors and use the trolling motor to get directly above the fish before setting the hook. Many times putting a little pressure on the fish raises it high enough to see what size it is and whether it has the bait fully in its mouth. A firm, sweeping hook set works the best. Try to keep the rod low

and pointed at the fish. When you do set the hook, make sure it is hard and to the side. Over-the-head hook sets may look good, but they won't get the job done and it leaves you in a bad position to react to the fish's next move.

As the water temperature falls below 50°F (10°C) swim a ³/4-ounce (20-g) jig tipped with any of the above-mentioned live baits over the tops of weed flats that are close to deep water. Also look for steep-breaking shorelines where the fish tend to cruise back and forth looking for food.

Anti-Spooking Tactics

In several of the lakes I regularly fish, the water is very clear and summertime muskie fishing can be tough. Some of the best muskie fishing I have had has been when the last Jet Ski has been put on the dock for the night and the lake calms down after being frothed by weekend boat activity.

I like to get out on the lake and be anchored and settled about half an hour before sundown. Once the sun is below the trees I cast my slip-bobber rig or jig and begin fishing late into the night. This also works from the bank, as muskies tend to move up on sandy flats near swimming beaches to feed on panfish.

When fishing from shore for pike or muskies, try to walk softly and stay out of the water if possible. In super-shallow water muskies can detect ripples and waves made by anglers walking in the water, which may keep them from coming into casting distance.

Once you hook a fish you can enter the water to release it. Remember that dragging fish up on the bank causes them great stress. For this reason I like to wear hip boots at all times when fishing from the bank.

Tips for Pike and Muskie

Use a paper punch on the plastic lid of a coffee can or use a piece of heavy rubber band to make small bait keepers for minnows and waterdogs tipped on your jig.

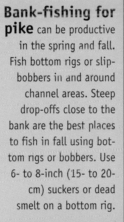

Bank-fishing for pike can be productive in the spring and fall. Fish bottom rigs or slip-bobbers in and around channel areas. Steep drop-offs close to the bank are the best places to fish in fall using bottom rigs or bobbers. Use 6- to 8-inch (15- to 20-cm) suckers or dead smelt on a bottom rig.

When using the size of bait that is required to attract trophy pike and muskies, you must give the fish time to eat the bait. Unfortunately, this increases the odds of a fish deeply swallowing the hook. Circle hooks and quick-strike rigs are designed to reduce this sometimes-fatal occurrence.

Largemouth Bass

I spend a great deal of time fishing for bass from the bank, boat and float tube. My favorite part of bass fishing is after the strong hook set, watching the line rise as the fish clears the water trying to throw the hook. When fishing in my float tube this often puts the fish right at eye level, with me getting my polarized glasses all wet—a great problem to have!

Where to Fish

With the help of television coverage, bass fishing's popularity is at an all-time high. Largemouth bass are a favorite throughout the U.S. and southern Canada because they are found in so many lakes, rivers and reservoirs; they can be caught shallow or deep throughout the year; and they put up one of the best battles in freshwater fishing. Largemouths can be caught on many types of live bait during most of the year.

Equipment

I recommend using a 6- to 6½-foot (1.8- to 2-m) medium-heavy push-button, spinning or baitcasting rod and reel combo with a minimum of 10-pound-test (4.5-kg) line. When fishing heavy cover 20- to 25-pound-test (9- to 11-kg) line is common and superlines and braids can really shine in many situations.

Hook sizes range from a #4 live-bait hook for stitching crayfish to a big, weedless 5/0 hook for jumbo shiners. The trick is to use a hook large

Fishing with a slip-bobber allows you to control the depth your bait is set at, and cast with ease.

Hook a crayfish through the bony horn with a small, short-shank hook, size 4 or 6 for good success in the summer. Use a split-shot for weight, or no weight at all.

enough to penetrate through both sides of the bait.

As with other species it is important to have a good sinker selection ranging from 3/0 to #4 split-shot and 1/4- to 1-ounce (7- to 28-g) bullet- or egg-sinkers. Many sinker manufacturers are now producing specialty sinkers that have built-in rattles. I prefer these to standard sinkers when fishing on the bottom or in dark-colored water.

Spring

Early in the season, bass concentrate in shallow, weedy bays and on hard-bottom flats. In reservoirs they are found from the secondary points all the way to the back of creek arms looking for food. This is the perfect time to fish a slip-bobber rigged with a 1/4-ounce (7-g) plastic-bodied jig fished just above newly emerging weeds or brush. Tip the jig with a small sucker, shiner, jumbo leech, large nightcrawler or fat-head minnow. Casting jigs tipped with these baits allow you to cover more water, searching for areas holding good numbers of hungry bass.

Once you have located a group of fish you can slow down and fish a slip-bobber tipped with the same live bait as mentioned above. Fish are on the move while feeding before the spawn so don't be afraid to cover water looking for larger ones. At this time of the year the fishing often picks up on sunny afternoons after the shallows have had a chance to warm up.

When water temperatures climb to around 60°F (15°C), bass begin to spawn. Depending on water clarity bass typically spawn in depths of 12 inches (30 cm) to 6 feet (1.8 m) of water, often near some type of structure like a weed edge, boulder, log or dock. Male bass use their tails to fan out silt and loose gravel creating a spawning bed. Bass beds are easy to spot on sunny days as they appear as a light-colored circle about 2 feet (60 cm) in diameter.

Although catching spawning bass has caused controversy in many part of the country, studies have shown that if bass are released in the spot they are caught, the majority of them will continue with a successful spawn.

The best bet is to cast a bobber rig or jig past the bedding area, then reel it in so it rests in the middle of the bed. Bass, being very protective parents, soon attack the bait, defending the bed full of future offspring. Crawlers, minnows and large leeches get the job done. Quickly fight the hooked fish and return it to the water near its beds. If you notice a female that is actually laying eggs, it is best to go on to another fish.

Summer

During the summer months some bass live shallow. Large schools of fish, however, can be found using sunken humps,

Tips for Largemouth Bass

Try floating jig-heads when slip-sinker fishing with nightcrawlers or crayfish. They keep bait above the bottom where it is less likely to snag, and easier for fish to see. Use a slip-sinker rig with a 2- to 3-foot (0.6- to 1-m) leader.

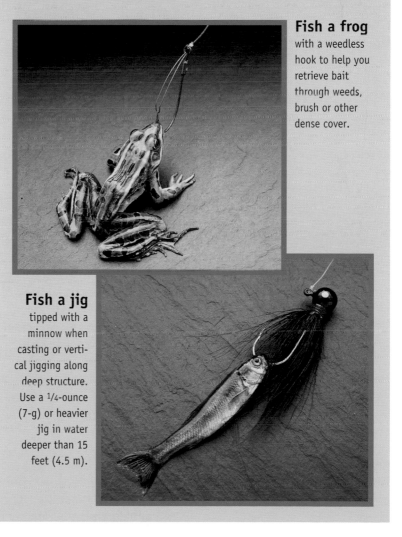

Fish a frog with a weedless hook to help you retrieve bait through weeds, brush or other dense cover.

Fish a jig tipped with a minnow when casting or vertical jigging along deep structure. Use a 1/4-ounce (7-g) or heavier jig in water deeper than 15 feet (4.5 m).

When fishing shallow water for all species of fish a good pair of polarized sunglasses is a must. As a second pair I recommend vermilion lenses, which work best in cloudy or low-light situations.

main-lake gravel or weedy points, turns in creek arms and deep timber. Cast jigs along the edges of these structures tipped with shiners, suckers and leeches. Fish crawlers, crayfish and leeches on a slip-sinker, Carolina rig or drop-shot rig. You will catch more fish if you drift vertically or cast along these likely haunts and try to locate schools of bass. I religiously use a GPS unit to mark these main-lake spots once I have found them because schools of bass use these areas throughout the summer; in some cases, year after year.

Shallow bass in the summer seek out dense weed or brush cover with access to deep water nearby. You can slip-bobber-fish with golden shiners, frogs, medium-size suckers or salamanders around these areas.

You can also freeline fish, which is a technique used by live-bait anglers in shallow water. Simply cast a plain hook with your favorite live bait and feed line to the bait, allowing it to swim naturally through the water. Concentrate on areas along structure that are likely to hold the gamefish you are after.

My favorite public bass lake in Minnesota is Lake Minnetonka; I've fished it regularly for twelve years now. The deeper, summertime areas where I located and caught bass in my first year of fishing the lake can still be very good producers.

A good portion of my summer bass fishing is at the competitive level. Unfortunately, most bass tournament rules do not allow live bait to be used. And I will be the first to tell you that the worst thing to see sitting on my starting spot is some good live-bait anglers with a couple dozen leeches or golden shiners. I just know they are catching bass!

In the southern U.S., a common fishing method is to use a balloon to float large shiners off the bottom, which allows them to roam along the edge of emergent weed mats. After a strike is detected and the fish has been given time to take the bait, anglers set the hook hard, popping the balloon or simply reeling it up, which gives them a direct line to the fish. Using the balloon replaces a standard bobber but your rig is more streamlined in heavy cover.

Be sure to use tackle heavy enough to pull fish from these watery jungles once they are on—20-pound-test (9-kg) line is a minimum. I use a heavy-action 7- or 7 1/2-foot (2.1- or 2.3-m) baitcasting rod and reel

combo with a long straight handle, which provides leverage to get fish out of heavy cover.

You can also pitch crawlers, leeches or minnows on bobber rigs and jigs into pockets in the cover. Let the bait sit for a minute or two and then repeat the process in the next pocket. Several fish can be caught from one pocket. The large mouth of a bass allows it to effectively prey on baitfish that can be 10 inches (25 cm) or bigger. Bass in southern waters can grow to weigh well over 10 pounds (4.5 kg), whereas a 6-pounder (2.7-kg) in the northern part of their range is a true trophy.

Docks can also be a good place to look for bass during the summer months, especially on heavily developed lakes or reservoirs. Skip or pitch a 1/8- or 1/4-ounce (3.5- or 7-g) skirted jig with a jumbo leech or minnow under and around docks. Let the jig settle to the bottom and slowly hop it back to the boat. You have to deal with some picking from panfish, but the steady weight of a good-size largemouth will not be mistaken for a small panfish. Be sure to cast under the dock or along the sides where the tires are located on a roll-in dock system. And don't forget to fish the swim ladder.

Floating docks, which are commonly used in reservoirs, can be fished with a split-shot rig tipped with a shiner, shad or leech. Use heavy tackle and line for dock fishing. Try to remember that your line and jig will be coming in constant contact with metal objects like chains, support poles, axles and swim ladders. Once you have located a good stretch of docks, the location should be good year after year, provided the water level is relatively the same. Many times the owner of the dock is surprised to see that big bass are living right under the dock. Remember to use courtesy when fishing near docks that are being occupied.

Fall

As with many other species, fall is one of the best times to catch a trophy largemouth bass moving to the shallows to feed before winter. Pitch bobber rigs or freeline with frogs, waterdogs, suckers and shiners in pockets around docks, lily pads, hyacinth and submergent shallow weeds. Key in on hard-bottom areas featuring sand, gravel and rocks, around channels, docks and flooded timber. These areas tend to have warmer water temperatures as they absorb heat from the sun throughout the day.

Bass are on the move during this time of year and many of the fish move to shallows. Schools can be found, however, on secondary points and inside turns of breaklines that have green weeds and a hard bottom. Don't be surprised if one day you catch fish deep on a spot and the next day they're gone— that's fall fishing so you have to cover water. Fish a slip-sinker or Carolina rig on the bottom along the weed edge tipped with a sucker, shiner, waterdog, jumbo leech or red-tail chub.

Autumn is when baitfish tend to be larger. I like to increase the size of all the live baits I use whenever possible. This means that you may have to let the fish take their bait for a longer period of time. If you are a catch-and-release angler or just like to avoid gut-hooking fish, try a circle hook at the end of your slip-sinker rig next fall.

When fishing heavy cover like logs, weeds, docks and even rock piles do yourself a favor and regularly check your line and knot for nicks and abrasions. "When in doubt, retie." That is the motto I live by. Also, many of the fish-holding objects dull a brand-new hook in just a few hours of fishing, so take out your file and touch it up often.

Smallmouth Bass

Smallmouth bass are the bronze-colored members of the bass family that are known for their tough fighting ability and their propensity to be in one spot one day and gone the next.

To consistently catch smallies you must understand where you are likely to find them and what live bait to pitch at them. As much as any other gamefish, the smallmouth bass is a perfect candidate for fishing with live bait.

Where to Fish

Smallmouths are found in streams, rivers, lakes and reservoirs across the U.S. and southeastern Canada. Smallmouth fishing can be some of the most addicting fishing you ever do. I think this fish is so popular because it is so unpredictable. If you catch three smallies, the first one will bulldog you to the end, trying to get to the bottom; the very next one will leap from the water too many times to count; and number three will run straight under the boat!

Spring

Smallmouths migrate to shallow, rocky or sand-gravel flats in the spring when water temperatures reach 60°F (15°C). This is one of the few times during the year that smallmouths are not too particular about what they hit. I've caught them on crawlers, fathead minnows, crayfish and leeches. My favorite springtime smallie bait is a jumbo leech fished on a slip-bobber rig or tipped on a 1/8- to 1/4-ounce (3.5- to 7-g) jig. The constant wriggling of that jet-black leech is just too much for a hungry smallmouth!

Because smallmouths prefer clear water in lakes and reservoirs, they seek out objects like boulders, logs, docks and buoys to provide the security needed to build their spawning beds.

Stream and river smallmouths spawn in slow current areas with sand or gravel bottoms. During spawn smallmouths become very aggressive, making them one of the easiest fish to catch while they are spawning.

The spawn, however, is a small window of opportunity for anglers, lasting only several days some years. Smallmouths typically turn a very dark brown while spawning, making them easy to spot on their beds if you have a good pair of polarized glasses.

A jumbo leech is still my favorite bait for this time of year, but it really does not matter what you use as long as you can get your bait near the bed. After the spawn, smallmouths head out to deeper water for the summer where you can find them concentrated around rocky humps, main-lake points, sunken objects (man-made or natural) and dock systems that are in or near deep water.

Using an underwater camera in a lake several years ago, I found a 20- by 15-foot (6- by 4.5-m) dock system sunk in 24 feet (7.25 m) of water that must have been blown into the lake during a storm. Suspended all around the dock were smallmouth bass—they just love to be around objects and near a hard bottom.

In spring, smallmouth move into shallow water to spawn. Use polarized sunglasses to spot them.

Summer

As far as bait choices go, chubs, crawlers, leeches and crayfish work very well in the summer. You can fish them on a slip-bobber rig, tipped on the back of a jig, or on a live-bait rig. Depending on the structure where they are holding you can fish vertically or cast along the edges of structure. One of my most productive ways to catch them is on a bottom bouncer or Carolina rig.

Using a $1/2$- or $3/4$-ounce (14- to 20-g) weight (make sure you have enough weight to stay in good contact with the bottom) and the bait of your choice from the list above, troll or drift the edges of likely structure. One thing that is nice about smallies is that when you do catch one, typically it is not alone. Because of this, be sure to cover the area well before moving on. Smallies are often found on one little section of a big rock pile or other large piece of structure.

If regulations allow you to fish with crayfish during the mid-summer period (and crayfish are the food base in the lake or river you are fishing), it's the best choice. In lakes with a minnow-based forage, minnows may keep the fish high off the bottom and not tuned in to a crayfish on the bottom.

A good place to fish for smallmouths with live bait is in rivers and streams. You can fish with chubs, crayfish, leeches, crawlers and insects around large boulders, eddies, logjams and riffles leading into deeper pools. When fishing rivers from a boat or canoe cast jigs tipped with a chub or leech at the bank and slowly bring it back. Or you can anchor your boat and fish a slip-sinker rig on the bottom in deeper holes, behind large boulders or anything that creates a current break. Another option for small rivers and streams is to wade-fish, either in waders or a pair of shorts in the warm months. I like to use a split-shot and live-bait hook tipped with a leech, crawler or minnow. My favorite technique is to cast it upstream of a deeper pool and let it drift until my line is directly below me, then repeat the process. I bring plenty of split-shot and hooks as the rocky haunts smallmouths love so much can be very snaggy but worth the work.

When smallies aren't very aggressive, try switching to insects like hellgrammites, stoneflies or crickets. Many times, using insects can turn the day around. In this situation you can fish for them on spinning tackle with a clear casting bubble or on a 6- or 7-weight flyrod with a small split-shot. Allow the insect to drift

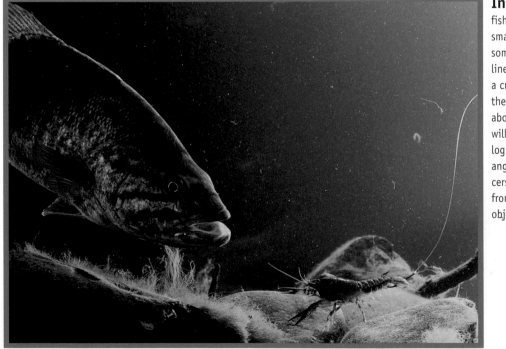

In summer, crayfish are a favorite of smallmouth bass. Keep some tension on your line when freelining with a crayfish. If you allow the crayfish to move about as it pleases, it will crawl under a rock or log and hide. Some anglers remove the pincers to keep the crayfish from holding onto objects on the bottom.

through riffles above deeper pools, along undercut banks or shoreline with boulders, or past overhanging trees.

Fall

Autumn is the time when some of the best smallie fishing can be had and may be the best time of the year for a trophy.

In lakes, smallmouths migrate to channels, docks and inlets flowing into the lake. These areas tend to attract baitfish and the smallies follow. Fish these areas with slip-bobber rigs tipped with a small to medium sucker or chub.

If you try fishing shallow without much luck, be sure to check for schools of smallmouth that are still out on rock piles and off the ends of main-lake points. Drift or troll a slip-sinker or Carolina rig tipped with a crayfish, chub or sucker around these areas to locate schools. Smallmouths

like to roam, so if they are not where you left them the last time you were out don't be alarmed, just widen the area you're fishing.

River and stream smallies will be on or near the shore in the fall; look for them near slack-water areas or rocky shorelines near deep water. As winter draws near smallies spend more time in deep pools and less time on shoreline structure. Whether you're anchored or wade-fishing these deeper pools, drift a split-shot or slinky rig through them with a medium sucker or chub. Once you have located a pool they are using, you'll have a late-fall smallmouth spot for years to come, as they tend to use the same pools year after year. If a dam is present in the system you are fishing, be sure to fish the deep-water areas both above and below the dam in the fall.

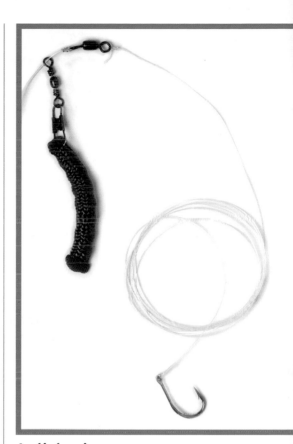

A slinky rig greatly reduces the number of snags you encounter. That makes it the perfect rig for fishing around rocks and other obstructions on the bottom.

When fishing smallmouth in large schools, several fish may follow a hooked fish to the boat trying to get any scrap of food the hooked fish may shake free during the fight. This is a good indicator of how many fish are in the area.

Catfish and Bullheads

Although these two species may look alike, they definitely are held in different regard when you hear anglers talk about them.

If someone tells you they are "only" catching bullheads, the initial reaction is to go to another lake or at the very least go to another spot. Whereas if an angler tells you he or she is catching catfish, the response is often Where? How big? How many? and What are you catching them on?

Bullheads are the smaller of the two species and seldom grow to over 1 pound (0.45 kg). On the other hand, catfish often weigh over 5 pounds (2.25 kg) and can top out at more than 100 pounds (45 kg). Catfish are a more challenging foe, which may also explain the disdain anglers have toward bullheads.

Catfish

Once summer rolls around where I live, water levels stabilize and warm to around 60°F (15°C) in the rivers. I get the itch to load up the jon boat with lanterns and camping gear on yet another quest for cats. Found throughout the U.S. and portions of southern Canada in lakes, rivers, bayous, ponds and reservoirs, catfish rank third in fishing popularity, after only panfish and bass.

The three most common species are channel catfish, blue catfish and flathead catfish. The flatheads and blues are the heavyweights of the bunch, often topping out near 100 pounds, while channels over 20 pounds (9 kg) are considered large. All three species use an acute sense of smell and use the many taste buds that are found in the barbels near their mouths to find food. Channel cats and blues can be caught on live bait like worms and insects, but most are caught with cut-bait or other catfish concoctions. Flatheads, on the other hand, are most often caught with live baits.

Where to Fish

Most good river catfish spots have one thing in common: some type of brush or sunken logjam known as a snag. These snags, preferably near hard-bottom deep holes, create a current break and ambush point for cats. Current seams, slack water near dams and eddies along riprap banks are also likely areas to find catfish. When the water is high or rising, fish eddies or snags, which provide a current break along the shore. Many of these types of spots can be fished from the bank; others may require a boat.

Catfish in large rivers and reservoirs can be a little harder to consistently locate because they—like most fish—follow the food. In the spring search

Fishing near snags is the key to catching catfish in rivers. These fish are solitary creatures, and a single spot of cover usually yields only one, at most two or three, adult fish.

around snags in the back of creek arms of reservoirs or running sloughs and backwaters off the main channel in large river systems. Large flats covered with snags adjacent to deeper holes or creek channels are good places to start fishing during the summer months in these larger systems. You may find that the concentration of cats is holding near inside turns and points along these holes or channels. Rock piles adjacent to these flats tend to be a magnet for cats because they often hold crayfish. And a crayfish to a catfish is like candy to a kid!

In high- and murky-water situations caused by excess rain, catfish can be caught during the day, but serious catfish anglers set up in the afternoon and fish long into the night when cats bite best and catching a trophy is more likely. The trick to any successful catfish trip is preparation; items such as headlamps, mosquito spray and plenty of organization will greatly increase the fun factor.

Equipment

My favorite catfish partner likes to say, "Any medium-heavy- to heavy-action 6- to 8-foot (1.8- to 2.4-kg) spinning or baitcasting rod is a good cat rod." The key is to be sure to invest in a good reel with an adequate drag system. When fishing for smaller catfish, 15- to 20-pound-test (6.25- to 9-kg) line works well. For larger cats 30-pound-test (13.5-kg) and larger is a must. In the past I have mainly used monofilament line, but the abrasion resistance, low diameter and lack of stretch of the new superlines have won me over for fishing in areas with large cats.

Live-bait hooks ranging from #1 to 6/0 are the best option, depending on the size of bait you are using. Always remember to bring a good selection of sinkers, 3/0 to #2 split-shot and 1/2- to 2-ounce (14- to 56-g) eggs or pyramids should cover most situations. Because of the habitat that catfish prefer, snagged lines and break-offs are common.

Bait

As far as bait goes, dough-baits, stink-baits, dip-baits, crawlers, chicken liver and oil-based cut-bait such as herring, suckers or shad work best on smaller channel cats and blues. They also have been known to catch larger fish in some cases. Flatheads are typically caught on live bait.

I recommend a slip-sinker rig or paternoster rig to get started, regardless of whether you are fishing from a boat or the bank. Both of these rigs allow cats to freely take line after a strike has been detected. Drifting rigs like a split-shot rig

Ways to Use Cut-Bait

Fillet, steak or cut slits in a whole bait to make the best use of its scent trail. When filleting, leave the skin on for better hookability (top left). If you chunk a medium to large baitfish into numerous smaller pieces (above), be sure to save the head. If you wish to use a whole, smaller baitfish, slice it several times on each side (bottom left).

Slip-sinker rig

Paternoster rig

or dropper rig work well to cover smaller holes or floating across flats in a boat. Use float rigs to cover lots of water when fish are spread out or suspended, or if you want to drift bait in the current. If you are like me and just like to watch a bobber dance along a current seam, float rigs get the job done.

When faced with unstable weather after a good rain, or when fishing for heavily pressured fish, try switching to large grasshoppers, catalpa worms, mayflies, live frogs or crayfish. Many large cats have been caught with these smaller-than-average baits. Be sure to penetrate the hook in the correct position to ensure smaller fish won't pick your bait clean before it has a chance to tempt a nice-size cat.

Large blues and flatheads acquire fairly refined diets in their old age, requiring anglers to use the freshest bait possible—cut-bait for blues and channels, live bait for flatheads. Ask your local tackle shop owner or guide what the main forage of catfish is in the body of water you plan to fish. If regulations allow try to purchase or catch that species of live bait prior to heading out to fish. Avid catfish anglers catch

bait no more than a few days before their next adventure to ensure its freshness.

In the southern U.S., large herring and shad are caught with cast nets or dip nets and either cut or fished live for big cats. In the North, large suckers are readily available and seem to work best because they are very hardy once they are hooked and give off good cat-attracting odor when used for cut-bait. I have used smelt and other oily baitfish, but the availability of large suckers and the fact that they are found naturally in most catfish waters make them common in most bait stores throughout the year. These large baitfish, whether cut or alive, are usually fished on the bottom with slip-sinker rigs or paternoster rigs, allowing the odor to fill the surrounding area in hopes of luring a giant cat.

Slip-sinker rigs and Paternoster rigs allow fish to take your bait and swim away with it, without feeling any resistance from the weight.

Jugging and Trotlining

Jugging, which is practiced primarily in the southern U.S., allows anglers to fish large areas in reservoirs and slow-moving rivers. The bait is hooked onto evenly spaced hooks along a heavy drop line (50-pound/22.5-kg), in order to cover a large range of depths in the water column. The drop line is then attached below a plastic bottle or jug with a 2- to 3-ounce (56- to 85-g) sinker attached to the bottom of the line to keep it riding vertically.

A white or brightly painted milk jug or one-liter pop bottle works well. Anglers slowly troll upstream and let out several of these free-floating jugs at one time. After all the jugs are in the water anglers float with the string of jugs downriver waiting for one to bob violently or swim against the current indicating a fish has taken the bait.

The resistance of the jugs helps the fish hook itself so anglers are not required to set the hook. Anglers then motor over and land the fish using gloves in a hand-over-hand

motion. Jugs are prepared with several different lengths of drop line to fish different depths and the set depth is written on the jug for reference.

Trotlining, is yet another effective way to cover a likely catfish hot spot. A heavy nylon main line (600-pound-test/270-kg) is stretched horizontally across a likely catfish hole. Evenly spaced 1- to 2-foot (0.3- to 0.6-m) lines are tied to the main line with a hook on the end. The main line can range from 25 to 100 feet (7.5 to 30 m) with drop lines attached.

Ways to Set a Trotline

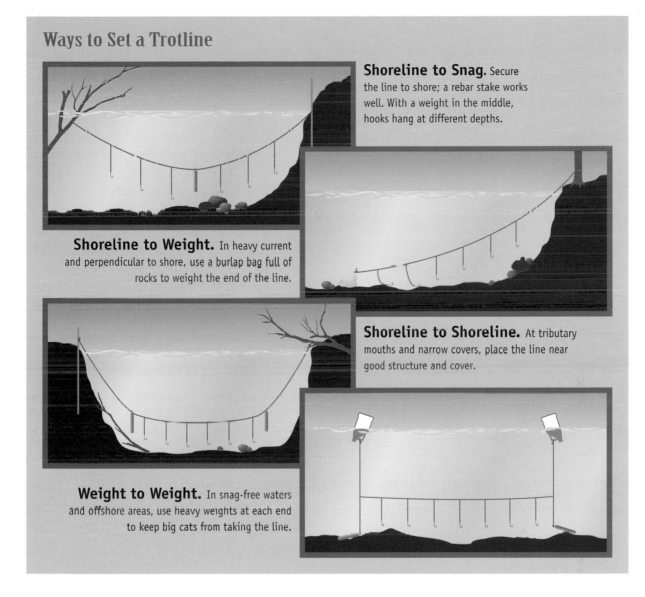

Shoreline to Snag. Secure the line to shore; a rebar stake works well. With a weight in the middle, hooks hang at different depths.

Shoreline to Weight. In heavy current and perpendicular to shore, use a burlap bag full of rocks to weight the end of the line.

Shoreline to Shoreline. At tributary mouths and narrow covers, place the line near good structure and cover.

Weight to Weight. In snag-free waters and offshore areas, use heavy weights at each end to keep big cats from taking the line.

Most trotliners set their spread during the day then bait them just before dark with sunfish, herring and other readily available bait. Setting them out just before dark keeps unwanted pests such as gar or turtles from cleaning the bait off the hooks in daylight. Anglers then check their trotlines in the morning. It is best to check trotlines with a buddy to run the boat. On a hot summer night when catfish are really feeding, the more hands available, the better.

Jugging

Watch for jugs that bob erratically or go under. Pursue them as they begin to swim away.

Grab the jug, not the line, to avoid cutting your hand on the line as the fish struggles.

Bullheads

Found in slow-moving rivers and shallow lakes and ponds bullheads are great fun to catch. When water temperatures reach 60°F (15°C) bullheads move to the shallows feeding on insects, worms, larvae and snails. They rely heavily on their acute sense of smell, plus taste buds located in their barbels to find food. (Barbels are the long whisker-looking appendages on the upper and lower lips of their mouths, oftentimes mistaken by anglers as stingers.)

Late spring and summer are the best times to fish for bullheads, when water temperatures climb to around 60°F (15°C). Bullheads bite throughout the day but the bite is best toward the evening hours. The same rod and reel used for panfishing work fine for bullheads also. You need a spincast combo or spinning combo with 6- to 10-pound-test (2.7- to 4.5-kg) line, a bag of 3/0 or #7 split-shot and some #8 or #10 long-shank hooks along with a few dozen angleworms or nightcrawlers. Because bullheads require very little oxygen, you can keep them for hours in a plastic pail filled with water.

Whether fishing from the bank or from a boat, I prefer to fish near some type of culvert, drain or inlet. Many times, especially after heavy rains, these inlets wash worms and other food into the lake, attracting good numbers of hungry bullheads to the area.

Simply pinch on a split-shot or two about 18 inches (45 cm) above the hook, thread on one or two whole worms and cast the rig, providing slack to allow the bait to settle to the bottom. Leave the button pushed or bail open on your reel to allow the fish to take line freely after it has taken the bait. After a few seconds set the hook—and the battle is on!

Bullheads are great to eat until about midsummer when high water temperatures cause the meat to become soft and possibly develop a muddy taste. Always handle bullheads with great care. They are equipped with a specialized barbed spine located in the dorsal and both pectoral fins. These spines are actually coated with a weak venom. While getting stung won't kill you, it will put a damper on the day.

Hold a catfish or bullhead by the bottom lip or behind the head. When you hold one behind the head, watch out for the sharp dorsal and pectoral spines, which can cause a painful wound.

Striped Bass and White Bass

When I think of stripers and white bass two words come to mind: fast and furious. They both spend much of their lives roaming open water feeding in groups, attacking schools of gizzard shad, threadfin shad and other baitfish. When this action is near the surface, they can put on an explosive show for anglers. Both species chase bait to the top of the water column with surges of speed, many times clearing the water's surface when they finally home in on a single baitfish. This explosion often sets off a chain reaction that spooks the rest of the baitfish in the area and they suddenly become targets for the frenzied fish below.

Unfortunately, this awesome display only lasts a short period of time in most cases and you have to be quick to react if you want to get in on the action. One of the telltale signs of this activity is seeing a large flock of seagulls feeding on injured baitfish near the surface.

Although these two species do have this feeding habit in common, stripers often grow up to ten times larger than their white relatives. There is also a hybrid cross between the two fish called a wiper, which tends to be somewhere in the middle as far as size goes. All three species often inhabit the same waterways and can be caught with similar methods. It is only the size of the gear and baits that has to change when you are concentrating on one species or the other.

White Bass will school together in large numbers to attack their prey, often pushing the bait to the surface where they can mount an attack.

Where to Fish

Stripers and white bass are most prevalent in large reservoirs in the central portions of the United States. Because they are both pelagic (open-water) species, they need large waters that contain large numbers of forage fish for them to feed on.

In the spring, both species move toward shallow water in the back of creek arms as they follow the baitfish that are attempting to spawn. Then they head back out to open water where they follow the prime food source.

A good locator is a must to have success with stripers and whites. The problem with these two species is that they often offer a boom-or-bust situation—you can catch them really well one day and come back the next day, only to find there are no fish around.

Locate white bass by looking for flocks of gulls. Use an electric motor to edge within casting distance of the school. If you run your outboard, the vibrations may spook the fish.

Equipment

To fish for white bass you need very basic tackle—these fish may weigh as much as 3 pounds (1.35 kg); the average is around 1 pound (0.45 kg). The best gear for whites is a 6- to 6½-foot (1.8- to 2-m) medium-power spinning or baitcasting combo with 8- or 10-pound (3.6- to 4.5-kg) monofilament line. I prefer to fish whites with ultralight spinning tackle and 4- to 6-pound (1.8- to 2.7-kg) monofilament to get the most fun I can out of these scrappy little fish.

If you are after white bass for the first time, first catch a bunch with medium-weight gear and then decide if you want to try to go to lighter gear. A bag of 3/0 and #7 split-shot works for a split-shot rig or slip-bobber. Live-bait hooks in size #2 or #1 cover most white bass fishing situations.

When fishing rivers bring extra hooks and sinkers, as you are bound to lose some to snags and the occasional wiper or striper that decides it needs your tackle more than you do. A good selection of ⅛- and ¼-ounce (3.5- and 7-g) plastic-bodied jigs or bucktail jigs in white or another bright color round out the tackle needed for a successful outing.

Striper tackle requires more hefty gear. I have seen what a 25-pound (11-kg) striper can do to an angler who has too light of tackle—it's not a pretty sight! A striper's ability to strike with great force and make hard, bulldogging runs toward deep water or snags requires anglers to use either light saltwater or heavy freshwater gear.

Spring

Stripers and white bass are easiest to catch in the spring when they migrate in large groups to the first upstream obstruction in streams, rivers and tributaries that feed lakes.

In reservoirs they congregate around the main-lake point, until the water temperature reaches about 55°F (13°C). At this time they migrate to the back of the creek arms where they attempt to spawn. But, of course, stripers cannot successfully spawn in reservoirs. They are actually a saltwater species that would naturally leave the saltwater in the spring to spawn in tributaries that feed into the ocean. Without these specialized spawning grounds, stripers do not reproduce. For this reason, nearly all stripers you find inhabiting an inland lake have been stocked into it.

Stripers and white bass that are found in rivers hold along slack-water areas like eddies, deeper holes, on inside bends of the river and behind other objects that create a current break close to the current of the main channel. These areas of slack water can be effectively fished from a boat or the bank.

Because white bass are not very finicky eaters, I like the cost effectiveness of a plain hook and a split-shot rig tipped with a crappie minnow, small shad or a larger baitfish cut into strips 1/2 by 2 inches (1.3 by 5 cm). With this setup, cast the rig upstream, allowing it to drift down through productive-looking slack-water areas. Add enough split-shot so you tick the bottom occasionally—too much split-shot and you'll be snagged for most of the day.

You can also use brightly colored jigs tipped with the same-size minnow or bait strip. In this case, cast upstream and swim the jig back to you, simulating an injured baitfish. I like white jigs when I fish in clear water and chartreuse ones when I fish darker water.

If the current or access to the spot does not allow you to effectively drift, a slip-sinker rig fished on the bottom is a good alternative. Position yourself or the boat above the slack-water area you are going to fish. Cast the slip-sinker rig downcurrent along the seam where the fast water meets the slack water. Feed line out to allow the sinker to settle to the bottom, making sure you have enough weight to hold on the bottom.

Keep the rod tip high enough to lift most of the line off the surface of the water. This helps reduce drag from the current and keeps weeds or other debris from collecting on the line. Tip the slip-sinker rig with a small shad, shiner, fathead minnow or nightcrawler. When faced with snag-filled, slack waters, a slip-bobber rig that is set to ride off the bottom will keep your bait and hook out of harm's way. Tip the slip-bobber rig with the same small minnow, shiner, shad or sucker meat strip that you would for the other applications.

The same methods as above are productive when fishing river stripers. When fishing from the bank be sure to familiarize yourself with the area surrounding the spot you are fishing. When a large striper is hooked you may need to follow it upstream or downstream to keep the fish clear of any line-breaking obstructions. Stripers are notorious for making drag-burning runs directly at objects

A Striper Lesson

On my first striper trip to Cumberland Lake in Kentucky I realized quickly how much respect the guide had for stripers. The guide's rods ranged from 6- to 7-foot (1.8- to 2.1-m) heavy-action, long-handled spinning and baitcasting rods with large-capacity reels loaded with 30- to 50-pound (13.5- to 22.5-kg) mono or superline. (I had a medium-power bass rod with 17-pound-test [7.6-kg] and was definitely under-geared for these salt-water transplants.)

As for hooks, all rods had heavy-wire live-bait styles ranging from 2/0 to 5/0 in size. The sinkers we used were from 1/4 to 1 ounce (7 to 28 g), depending on the depth of the schools of baitfish we spotted on the depth finder. Instead of bobbers we used balloons that were inflated to 3 inches (7.6 cm) in diameter and tied to the line.

The balloon was then adjusted so the bait would ride just above the depth of the baitfish clouds. Balloons have less resistance in the water and made it easier for the shad we were using to swim naturally.

At the first vicious strike the balloon popped, the rod loaded up and the fight was on!

White bass anglers commonly use a white jig with a strip of belly meat attached to the jig when fishing is slow. The piece of meat can measure about 1/4 by 1 1/4 inches (6 by 32 mm) long.

Using a Ballooon Rig for Stripers

Push the hook through a shad's nostrils. Use a 1/0 or 2/0 hook for 4- to 6-inchers (10- to 15-cm); a 3/0 or 4/0 for 7- to 11-inchers (18- to 28-cm). This hooking method keeps the shad lively.

Rig balloon lines using an overhand knot to tie the balloon at the proper depth. Add a large split-shot 4 feet (1.2 m) above the hook.

Troll with a bow-mounted electric motor so you can move quietly and avoid spooking fish.

in the water that slice the line. Knowing your surroundings ensures safe footing during the battle. Anglers fishing from boats simply pull anchor and follow fish while steering the boat clear of danger.

The size of baitfish used to target stripers will be considerably bigger than what is used for white bass. Use a 4- to 6-inch (10- to 15-cm) shad, shiner or sucker. You may be able to purchase the bait you need from the local bait store. Avid striper anglers use cast nets or dip nets to catch their own bait under the cover of darkness. Find a good pier or marina that has large lights set up at night and you should be able to catch enough bait for the next day. Catching your own ensures you have fresh bait that is the right size and is also much easier on the pocketbook!

At the minimum, 30-pound-test (13.5-kg) can be used to keep pressure on the fish at all times. I have found that 6½- to 7-foot (2- to 2.1-m) heavy-power baitcasting gear is really the only option for landing these fish.

Summer

After the spring shallow-water action tapers off, this is when stripers and white bass head back out to open water. In reservoirs, old creek channels, edges of sandy flats and mouths of major creek arms are likely areas to find roaming stripers and white bass all the way through the fall. The key to finding them is to keep track of the baitfish schools they are feeding on. Find the bait, and the fish will be nearby.

In river systems, search deep holes on inside bends of the

main channel, deep riprap banks with slow-moving current and points or wing dams that create a current break.

I once asked a guide what the secret was for his long record of success in catching stripers and white bass. His answer was simple: good electronics and covering water with a trolling motor or small gas-powered kicker motor in areas that hold baitfish.

If you like to troll, then you're going to love fishing for stripers and white bass. Slowly troll jigs tipped with sucker meat strips for white bass or, in many areas, the local bait shops have special spinner rigs that can be tipped with cut-bait.

Once you locate a large school of fish, cast or vertically jig your bait around the area to cover the school more thoroughly. White bass and stripers are always on the move. If the action slows, widen the area you are casting or vertically fishing until you relocate the school.

Trolling for stripers with live bait can be as simple as hooking a shad through the nostrils and freelining it behind the boat.

Avid striper anglers use planner boards, downriggers and balloons to cover a wider area and multiple depths at the same time. Planner boards allow anglers to run baits away from the boat, which can spook fish suspended near the surface. Downriggers are used when schools of fish are driven deep by sunlight or the heat of summer. Using balloons rigs as mentioned at the beginning of this section is simple; it keeps live shad at the proper depth and, of course, helps indicate a strike.

Fall

Once autumn arrives and water temperatures begin to fall, the nomadic summertime stripers move back toward the creek arms they used in the spring as they follow baitfish. Now that the water has cooled, stripers can use the entire water

column and are often found closer to the surface than they are in the summer. As you do with stripers in the spring, begin by looking for them near main-lake points and work your way back to the secondary points until you make contact with fish. As always, keep a close eye on your electronics to find the depth that the baitfish are using and concentrate your efforts around that depth.

Bait choice does not change, as the stripers are still focused on the baitfish schools for food. If you have access to live shad or whatever is prominent, freelining them and rigging them on balloon rigs are still the best options. Vertical jigging with large spoons and horse-head jigs tipped with sucker strips is also a fall favorite in many areas. This is a more aggressive approach that can really lead to large numbers of fish if you locate an active school. The scent of the sucker meat is often the key to getting bass to strike.

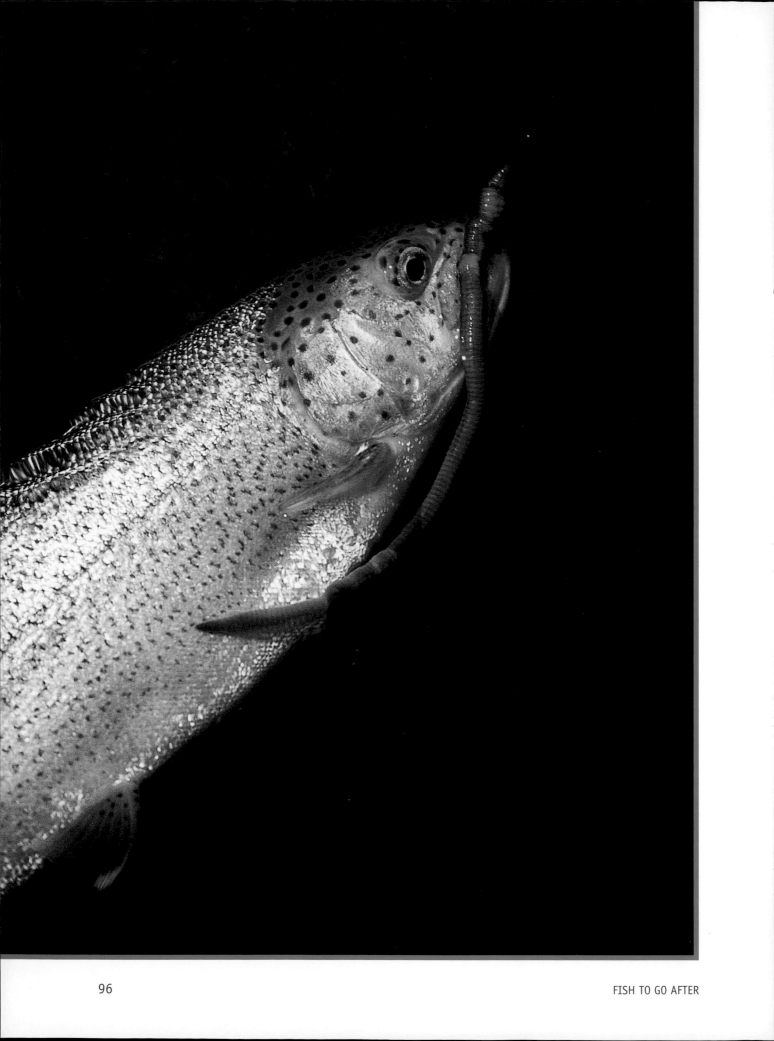

Trout

My first experience with trout was in my first year of high school. One of my teachers was an avid live-bait angler for stream trout. Every year on the opening weekend of trout season he would take a select group of students to his secret trout stream. Even though we arrived before the sun came up, I soon realized that his "secret" trout stream had been found by hundreds of other anglers who had camped out along the stream the night before.

I asked my teacher what was so secret about this stream. He replied by handing me a pair of hip boots and instructing, "Put these on and grab that 5-gallon (19-l) bucket." The older students had already obeyed and were heading to the stream; they already knew the secret.

As I reached the edge of the stream I witnessed a production line of students working in pairs. One would root around in shallow grassy clumps along the shore while the other was positioned downstream with a 4-foot-wide (1.2-m) seine.

"When are we going to fish?" I asked. All production stopped, the teacher walked up to me and handed me a handful of the secret—waterworms. "As soon as we get enough bait for all of us we can fish."

We caught lots of fish on the stream that day, and from then on I've been hooked on trout fishing. My passion for trout has taken me to many different parts of the country to experience numerous different types of trout fishing.

Where to Fish

Trout are found in streams, rivers, lakes, ponds and reservoir tailraces. Because all trout species need cool water to successfully reproduce, the fish found in ponds and lakes are stocked fish. Regardless of where you fish for trout, one thing is sure: They depend heavily on a diet of insects, crustaceans and baitfish to survive.

Pond and lake trout have a diet heavy with insects. Stream trout found in lakes may forage on more baitfish than insects because flowing cold water is required for many types of insects to be found in good numbers.

Equipment

An ultralight spinning outfit 5½ to 6 feet (1.7 to 1.8 m) long, spooled up with 2- to 6-pound-test (0.9- to 2.7-kg) monofilament line is what I use when fishing live bait for trout in streams or lakes. A 3- to 6-

Drift-fishing is the main method used for catching trout. The idea is to present your bait so it drifts naturally with the current. Almost any natural bait tough enough to stay on the hook will work.

Caddisworms are hooked in the head or threaded on a #12 to #16 light-wire hook. Some anglers use several worms, or the worm and case.

Aquatic insects like (1) stonefly nymphs, (2) hellgrammites, (3) mayfly nymphs, (4) caddis pupae and (5) water-worms will take trout year-round, but stonefly nymphs are best in midsummer; hellgrammites, in spring and early summer.

weight flyrod that is 8¹/₂ or 9 feet (2.5 or 2.7 m) in length with a floating line works well when fishing the moving water of streams or rivers.

Live-bait fishing with a fly-rod takes a little more practice to successfully present a bait. Keeping the bait on the hook long enough to entice a trout is the tricky part.

No matter how I fish for trout I always have a good selection of split-shot. I carry size B to #7 shot in a small plastic box with numerous com-partments. I prefer live-bait hook sizes #8 to #2, which cover most of the trout fishing situations I may encounter.

Clear-plastic casting bubbles and small slip-bobbers are needed for presenting insects and worms. The casting bubble allows you to cast weightless insects to hungry trout. Slip-bobbers work well when fish are suspended in lakes or when snags prevent the bait from being fished on the bottom.

Because trout prefer very

clean water, they can be pretty spooky when you're fishing small streams or lakes. One thing I like to do is to wear drab clothing and act more like I'm hunting than fishing when I'm searching for trout. Simply walking along the shoreline of trout waters can be enough to spook wary trout. I oftentimes resort to using fluorocarbon line when fishing ultraclear water. A pair of hip boots or waders is a must to seriously chase trout, as many of the best spots require you to cross a stream or stand in the stream to present the bait properly.

Bait

Angleworms, waxworms and insect larvae hooked on a plain hook with a split-shot is the best way to get started fishing for trout in streams. Position yourself below a shallow, rocky riffle that dumps into a deeper pool. Cast the split-shot rig up and across the top of the pool, then let the bait drift down through the length of the pool.

After a few casts, take a step downstream and repeat the process. Use enough split-shot so that it just ticks the bottom; if you're not getting caught on the bottom occasionally you're not using enough split-shot.

Use a slip-bobber rig and the same drifting method when fishing pools with very little current or covered with logs and trees. Set the bobber so the bait rides up off the bottom and use the rod to steer the bobber around any snags.

Insects found in and along the stream, such as grasshoppers, hellgrammites, stoneflies and waterworms, work equally well for bait but you must spend the time to catch enough of them. Insects for trout are hard to find in bait stores, which makes angleworms, waxworms and insect larvae, my top choices.

During the middle of the day when trout are less likely to be active, try a slip-sinker fished on the bottom and tipped with an angleworm, insect or larva.

This is known as "plunking" in some parts of the country. When using insects and larvae the current washes away the fish-attracting scent after awhile so be sure to change bait often. Spent bait looks as if it has been deflated and becomes soft and mushy.

If you're like me and like to be the first angler in the parking lot, you'll surely encounter trout rising to insects on the surface of the water. This phenomenon lasts for varied periods of time, depending on the time of year and weather.

Use a clear casting bubble tipped with one of the adult insects they are feeding on. In many cases the adult insects are too small to keep on a hook and present properly. If you have a small seine use it to catch the emerging insect larvae floating in the water for bait. When both the larvae and the adult insects are too small for a hook I recommend trying a single waxworm or larva.

Rising trout can be very

spooky so position yourself above the area they are rising. Cast and feed slack to the bubble and bait, letting it drift into the fish zone. A flyrod with floating line also works using the same method; the floating flyline eliminates the need for the bubble.

Rivers

When you have gained confidence in small streams and would like to venture to larger rivers where trout are found, a boat is necessary because the depth and current limits wading and access to fish-holding spots. The same methods you've used on small streams to catch trout work on bigger rivers; you'll just be doing it from a boat.

I only ask two things: Promise me you won't leave the house without at least one anchor in the boat and at least 50 feet (15 m) of good rope. The fast current in many large rivers keeps the boat moving at a rapid pace and anchoring

Terrestrial insects can be fished alive or dead, floating or submerged. (1) Hoppers and (2) crickets are hooked with a size 6 to 10 light-wire hook, either under the collar or through the body. (3) Waxworms are hooked through the head with a size 10 or 12 light-wire hook; some anglers hook on two or three.

allows you to cover areas thoroughly before moving on. A good set of rowing oars is also a must; the water is often too shallow to run a motor or restrictions limit the use of motors.

Stream trout in lakes come into shallow water during spring and fall to feed on baitfish when the water's surface temperature cools. If the water you are fishing has a tributary that flows in or out of it, start fishing in that area. Flowing water is cooler than stagnant main-lake water. Fishing from the bank is more productive during these cool-water periods because trout come within casting distance of the bank.

Slip-bobbers tipped with angleworms, larvae and small shiner or fathead minnows produce when fish are suspended, particularly early and late in the day or when skies are cloudy. During the middle of the day, use a slip-sinker rig fished on the bottom. I like to use a worm blower to keep a worm up off the bottom. Or, colored marshmallows (I prefer pink or orange to simulate the color of spawn) to float the bait off the bottom.

In rivers and streams big trout are historically caught from areas in and around the deepest holes. I like to use a split-shot rig for drifting and a slip-sinker rig when fishing on the bottom. Several good holes can be found and fished throughout rivers or streams. Drift-fishing allows anglers to cover more water, which increases the odds of locating a big fish.

Pay close attention while fishing in the morning and evening, as big trout often show themselves while rising on an insect. I have also had them chase my bait as I reel it in, or seen them chasing minnows and small trout. Later in the day I always return to the pool where the big fish was spotted and cast a slip-sinker rig in hopes of tempting it to bite.

Unfortunately, anglers must catch much of the baitfish they need for catching big browns and rainbows. The list of my favorites includes sculpins, chubs, suckers, shiners and fathead minnows. One bait that is often overlooked for big browns is crayfish—try drifting one through the deepest pool on the stream you are fishing and hold on!

Tips for Plunking

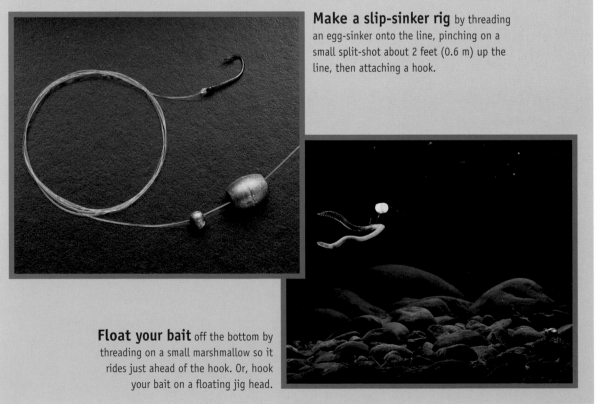

Make a slip-sinker rig by threading an egg-sinker onto the line, pinching on a small split-shot about 2 feet (0.6 m) up the line, then attaching a hook.

Float your bait off the bottom by threading on a small marshmallow so it rides just ahead of the hook. Or, hook your bait on a floating jig head.

Lakes

As the water warms in lakes, many trout head out to deeper, cooler water while following baitfish. On smaller lakes float tubes and small rowboats get you out to the fish. Cast and retrieve split-shot rigs and small jigs tipped with worms, shiners or fathead minnows. Cover lots of water; stream trout in small lakes use structure but often roam in open water off the structure instead of holding on points and sunken islands like other gamefish do. Look for fish or bait with a fish locator to determine the depth of the fish.

Bigger bodies of water like the Great Lakes—where brown and lake trout are common—require large fishing boats with sophisticated electronics and navigational devices to ensure safety. Trolling and drifting to cover water is the best way to find these open-water trout.

To keep live bait down at the depth where fish are spotted on the depth finder use cowbells, dipsey divers and downriggers. When trolling for trout in large lakes use nightcrawlers, smelt and sucker meat strips with the skin left on for durability. Once you have located fish try vertical jigging over the school with 1- to 2-ounce (28- to 56-g) bucktail jigs tipped with smelt or sucker meat. Trout can be caught in depths of 100 feet (30 m) and greater.

Big rainbow and brown trout generally need to feed on larger food than insects to maintain their body mass. But they still take advantage of a good insect hatch as a source of food. Rigging baitfish, however, is my favorite way to target large trout.

Undercover Fishing

I once took a trip with my best friend and flyfishing mentor out to the Big Horn River in Montana. We brought several fly-rods but we had covertly stashed our spinning rods in our flyrod tubes. This was hard for my friend to do since he has become a celebrity in purist flyfishing circles of the Upper Midwest; thus, the reason I am not going to mention his name.

We arrived late in the morning after a fifteen-hour drive and headed down to the river armed with our usual flyrods and waders. The water was much higher than normal for that time of the year and flyfishing was tough, but we caught some fish.

After a much-needed good night's sleep, we were ready for our first full day of fishing. We stashed our spinning rods in the drift boat along with all our fly gear and headed down the river. At the end of the day when the sun was on the treetops and the take-out point was in sight we decided to pull onto a sandbar so we could wade-fish. Out came the spinning rods.

Up to this point in the day we had been fishing with flies and streamers and were catching fish but no big ones yet. Using live bait was out of the question while in the presence of my friend, so minnow imitations had to do.

So there I am in the middle of this giant river trying to steady myself in the current and cast a minnow bait. The whole time I kept looking over my shoulder to see if any fly anglers were coming around the bend and might see me using a spinning rod. Sure enough, after a few casts I hooked a large rainbow. And my friend sees another drift boat approaching. He shouted to me to hide my rod.

I didn't think so! I hadn't driven fifteen hours across two states to lose a large trout because my friend was worried about being caught breaking the cardinal sin of a flyfishing purist.

I landed that 20-inch-plus (50-cm) fish and commenced catching several others before it was too dark to see.

When we arrived back at camp many of the anglers—or should I say "flyfishing purists"—found the conditions less than ideal, and the number of fish caught was disappointing. I had to just smile and keep my mouth shut.

Salmon and Steelhead

If you plan to fish for salmon and steelhead aboard a boat in large lakes and reservoirs you will need to be patient and cover a lot of water to find these open-water species. Many times both salmon and steelhead will be caught on the same trolling pass, just at different depths. Steelhead will typically be caught higher in the water column than salmon.

Shore fishing for these species in the tributaries that feed large lakes, oceans and tailraces of reservoirs may be some of the most challenging experiences you will ever encounter.

Steelhead typically migrate into spawning tributaries during the spring. On the coastal U.S. and in some tributaries of the Great Lakes you will find a fall run of fish also. Salmon migrate up tributaries from late summer through the fall, providing shore anglers an opportunity to catch them before they spawn and die.

One thing to remember when fishing for salmon and steelhead: Persistence pays off. It may take a few outings before you have what you consider a good trip but I guarantee after you hook your first salmon or steelhead you never forget it. These are the hardest fighting fish I have caught in freshwater. I spent one summer guiding for salmon in Alaska, and I can attest that the fishing is truly unbelievable!

Salmon

I began fishing for Chinook and pink salmon when I was a senior in high school while working at a local bait and tackle store. Every fall, when salmon were heading up the rivers on the north shore of Lake Superior to spawn, salmon anglers would come out of the woodwork looking for gear to catch their favorite quarry.

During the summer months we had a lot of customers who trolled the Great Lakes for salmon and lake trout using artificial spoons and plugs aboard big boats, armed with numerous electronics. They were generally well-to-do business types who were headed out on a charter and wanted to get their own gear because they could afford higher quality rods and reels than were provided. They also picked up the hot-color spoon that a friend had used on an earlier trip, and recommended.

In fall, however, the salmon anglers I helped in the store seemed to be a different breed—mainly blue-collar, hearty-looking individuals. Many of them had a look in their eye that I didn't see with our typical panfish and walleye customers. These customers were on a mission; it was as if there was a gold rush going on and they wanted to get their share.

I decided I needed to know what salmon fishing was all about. So with borrowed gear, some friends from the store and I piled into a car and headed north to the tributaries of Lake Superior. When we arrived at the first river we were going to fish, I put on my hip boots and followed the group to the river. I couldn't believe my eyes; there were at least a hundred anglers lining the shores of the river, all standing right next to each other. Each one of them had the same look as the customers in the store.

Fishing was poor for our group that day. But the entertainment of it all had a lasting impact on me. We watched angler after angler get snagged, tangle with each other and fight fish that would run downstream forcing other anglers to get out of the way.

I learned from one of the guys in our group that this was known as combat fishing. The competitive nature of these anglers was fierce, guarding their 4-foot (1.2-m) spot along the shore practically to the death. For some odd reason this was intoxicating to me even though the fishing was poor.

Salmon fishing in the tributaries of Lake Superior has changed a lot since then. Depleted populations of salmon and restrictions on the catch have reduced the number of anglers. So the true days of combat fishing aren't like they once were. Numerous anglers still flock to the rivers in the fall to try their hand at catching salmon, but the anglers are a more diverse group, many of them with stream trout fishing in their background.

Where to Fish

The Pacific salmon family includes Chinook, Coho, pink, sockeye and chum. They are found in rivers and streams on the West Coast from northern California to Alaska. They migrate up the same rivers they were born in to spawn and then die.

Atlantic salmon are found in streams and rivers along the East Coast from New York to Labrador. Unlike Pacific salmon,

Salmon fishing can be done from shore, particularly when the fish are staging in front of feeder streams or rivers prior to spring or fall runs.

Atlantic salmon migrate up streams to spawn, then return to the ocean and repeat the process several times throughout their lives.

The Great Lakes also have large populations of salmon that were first stocked successfully in 1966. Good numbers of Chinooks are also found in North Dakota's Lake Sakakawea and South Dakota's Lake Oahe. Other cold-water lakes in the West have been stocked with kokanee, the freshwater version of a sockeye. The cold, deep freshwater lakes of the Northeast have for years been stocked with Atlantic salmon.

Salmon spend most of their lives out in the open water of the ocean and the large fresh-water lakes they have been stocked in. Feeding on smelt, herring and other baitfish, they also prefer water temperatures ranging from 53°F to 57°F (12°C to 14°C). Ocean currents and wind currents in lakes cause salmon to constantly search for this preferred temperature. This means salmon may cover several miles in one day to stay in preferred water temperatures. Trolling with artificial lures during most of the year is how anglers catch these open-water salmon. From midsummer to early fall, the 3- to 4-year-old salmon migrate to the mouths of the tributaries where they were born to prepare to run up the river or stream to spawn.

For many salmon anglers this migration period marks the beginning of the season. Salmon can be caught from shore using live bait now because they are within casting distance for the first time during the year in most cases.

When water temperature and level are right, salmon begin entering the rivers. To me, this is when the season truly begins; I constantly monitor stream-flow gauges and message boards on the Internet for any sign of the first run of salmon.

Wade-fishing for salmon in streams and rivers is some of the most challenging fishing I do. This is because where I live in Minnesota the runs are smaller and depend heavily on rainfall. Over the years I have spent a ridiculous amount of time chasing fish reports because the closest river to me is three hours away. If you are fortunate to live near a good salmon river you can monitor it by simply driving down to the first upstream boundary to see what's going on. The Internet has helped minimize the number of trips I take only to find no fish in the river, mainly due to low water. Fish come into many tributaries along the Great Lakes after a good rain in the fall and drop back out of the lake if the water levels become too low. Larger rivers with a more sustained water flow do not pose this problem.

Equipment

To fish for salmon in streams and rivers you need to dress warmly and have a good pair of waders. Salmon hold and rest in deep pools, deep slots along steep banks and in large pools created by dams or naturally occurring waterfalls. Here's a tip for using a 9-foot (2.7-m) #8 flyrod and reel combo: Instead of flyline, spool the reel with 12-pound (5.4-kg) mono. To the end of the 12-pound line slip on a slinky and then tie on a #12 barrel swivel. To the swivel attach a 3-foot (1-m) piece of 6- or 8-pound (2.7- or 3.6-kg) mono and snell a #2 egg hook to the end of it—this is a drift rig. Tip the hook with a spawn bag and you're all set.

This method also works with an 8- or 8¹/₂-foot (2.4- or 2.6-m) spinning rod. When fishing larger rivers a spinning rod with a slip-bobber and a #2 hook tipped with a spawn bag works well. Cast the bobber upstream and let it drift back past you. Reel in any excess slack as the bobber floats by. Small brightly colored jigs

How to Tie a Spawning Bag

Place a chunk of spawn or several large, single eggs on a 2- to 3-inch square (5- to 7.6-cm) of red or white nylon mesh. A nylon stocking works well.

Pick up the corners of the nylon mesh. Carefully gather them in one hand to form a spawn bag ³/₈ to ⁵/₈ inch (9.5 to 16 mm) in diameter.

Wrap five loops of thread around the gathered mesh. Make sure the bag is formed tightly around the eggs.

Pinch the loops so they will not unravel. Tie a series of half-hitches to secure the bag.

Trim excess materials. Drop the bag into a glass jar containing borax, and shake the jar to coat the bag. Refrigerate up to two weeks, or freeze.

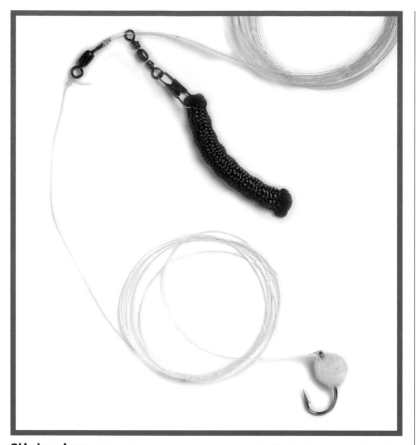

Slinky rig flexibility allows anglers to present a bait effectively when dueling with rocks and currents—with less of a chance of getting snagged.

also work with a spawn bag if the water is murky from recent rains.

When using a flyrod you're not actually flyfishing because you're using the weight of the flyline to cast the drift rig. As with trout fishing, position yourself at the head of a pool, strip 20 feet (6 m) of line off the reel and flip the rig slightly upstream. Lock the rod butt under your forearm and use the length of the rod to keep the line off the water as you follow the bait down. After repeated casts take one step down and repeat the process.

Use a big enough slinky so you can feel it ticking the bottom as it drifts down through the pool. When the bait stops or hesitates even a little, set the hook. Spawn bags are fairly durable but the rocky bottoms found in most salmon rivers take their toll. So be sure to change the bag when it appears to be deflated and mushy.

Salmon Challenge

I use an 8½-foot (2.6-m), two-piece medium-light-action spinning rod with at least 250 yards (228 m) of 10-pound (4.5 kg) mono when fishing from shore for salmon.

If conditions allow, I wade out up to my waist and cast a slip-sinker rig tipped with a fresh spawn bag as far out as possible. The long rod allows a cast much farther than traditional gamefish rods and the added length is needed for a good hook set.

After the bait has settled on the bottom I leave the bail open and head back to shore. I use some type of rod holder (often called a Guthery) to prop the rod up and wait for a strike—it's a lot like catfishing in many ways. A small float threaded on the line before I tie on the hook helps float the bait up off the bottom. I use a #2 size live-bait hook. (I'm not too particular with the color but red and green seem to work well.)

While the rod is propped up, I leave the bail open on the reel, allowing the fish to freely take line.

After a bite is detected I reel in all the slack line and wait until I feel the weight of the fish. Then I set the hook several times to ensure the hook point has good penetration. The drag must be set properly or the fight will be over as quick as it started. I try to have a friend grab the line at the end of the rod. I lift the rod tip until the rod feels fully bent; at this point the drag should release. I then loosen the drag ⅓ of a turn more and I'm ready to fish.

Live herring is used for bait on the West Coast, also fished on the bottom with a slip-sinker rig and float. Anglers in the Great Lakes and on the East Coast have had success with live ciscoes, stoneflies and nightcrawlers fished on the same rig. I like to use two large nightcrawlers hooked several times on a hook, which ends up looking like a ball or gob of worms.

Steelhead

Steelhead are rainbow trout that spend their adult lives out in the open water of the Pacific Ocean or large freshwater lakes like one of the Great Lakes. Each spring they return to the streams and rivers where they were born to spawn. Some rivers and streams have fish that migrate up them in the fall and winter until spring when they spawn. West Coast steelhead anglers can find fish in the rivers and streams during most of the year.

I use the same methods to catch steelhead as I do for salmon. However, because steelhead are in the trout family they can be caught using a wider variety of natural bait. Drift rigs and slip-bobbers can be tipped with the usual fare of night-crawlers and spawn but when fishing is difficult, due to clear water or unstable weather, stoneflies found along the river under logs and rocks can be deadly. Eurolarvae and waxworms on a small jig or plain hook below a slip-bobber can also produce fish in gin-clear water.

More so than salmon, steelhead hold in faster moving water while migrating up rivers and tributaries to spawn. Steelhead typically migrate after salmon have made their way into the rivers and spawned. This reduces the need for steelhead to compete for a spot in the gravel to spawn. Both salmon and steelhead spawn in shallow areas with gravel from 3 to 5 inches (7.6 to 13 cm) in diameter. These fish fan out an area 2 to 3 feet (0.6 to 1 m) wide and 4 to 6 inches (10 to 15 cm) deep for a bed, known as a "red." This is where they deposit their eggs.

Once steelhead and salmon have laid their eggs and begin guarding their reds they become very aggressive. Anglers should position themselves above spawning fish and float a slip-bobber with live bait or drift a slinky rig down and across the area. Using polarized sunglasses salmon and steelhead can be spotted from the bank on sunny days when the water is fairly clear. This helps anglers judge where to cast to ensure the bait drifts in front of the spawning fish. Be sure to wear drab-col-

ored clothing—if you can see the fish they can see you, and if you spook them they will be more difficult to catch.

Steelhead moving up the river in search of a prime spawning location hold in deeper runs below fast-moving riffles and behind large boulders. These and other objects in the water create pockets with a current break, which allows steelhead to rest before moving on to the next holding area. Drifting a slinky rig tipped with spawn, stoneflies or crawlers works best for fishing this faster moving deep water and pockets. Use enough weight on your slinky rig so that as you drift, your slinky is occasionally ticking the bottom.

Salmon also use these same pockets when migrating up the river but spend most of the time while in the river in the slower moving waters provided by large, deep pools and eddies. Many times these large pools and eddies are found where the river makes a turn or widens out. I recommend a slip-bobber tipped with spawn, stoneflies or nightcrawlers for fishing these slow-moving areas.

Chapter 5

Ice Fishing

All anglers should experience ice fishing at least once in their fishing careers. It is always a treat to take out someone who has never driven a car on the lake before, only to jump out, drill an 8-inch (20-cm) hole in the ice and start fishing. The facial expressions are worth the trip!

But ice fishing is much more than randomly drilling in the ice and hoping there are fish below.

Because the water temperatures are at their coldest this time of year, fish eat less often and are more selective in what they do eat. This is one of the main reasons that live bait is a must in most ice fishing situations. Traditional summer baits such as nightcrawlers and leeches are not available at the bait stores and do not perform well in these cold water temperatures anyway. The use of minnows and waxworms is pretty much the standard.

"I'll take a scoop of fatheads and a box of waxies" is a familiar request heard in bait shops in hard-water areas of the U.S.

and Canada. Fatheads, shiners, suckers and redtail chubs are the preferred minnow species when gearing up for larger fish on an ice adventure. Anglers most commonly use waxworms, spikes, mousses and eurolarvae to fish for panfish and trout through the ice, all of which are larval forms of various insects.

Equipment

Regardless of what species you fish for, some basic equipment is needed before heading out on the ice. Warm clothes worn in layers, well-insulated boots, gloves, sunglasses and a warm hat are must-haves. Then, you need an ice auger, either hand- or gas-operated.

An auger can cut a hole from 5 to 10 inches (12.7 to 25 cm) in diameter, depending on the size that best fits your needs. I recommend buying a 6-inch (15-cm) hand auger for early-season fishing when the ice is thinner. I prefer an 8- to 10-inch (20- to 25-cm) gas auger for chasing larger fish later in the season when the ice can be up to 4 feet (1.2 m) thick. After the hole is cut you need to clean the ice shavings from the hole created by the auger, so a scoop of some sort comes in handy.

Due to the high probability of harsh weather, I always fish from some type of shelter. Typically I use a portable one that is designed to double as a

sled for transporting all the gear onto the lake.

As far as actual fishing gear, an ultralight spinning reel is a good choice. It will freeze up less often than a spincast reel and can be set in a rod holder with the bail open to allow fish to take line freely after a strike. Ice rods, like summer rods, are available in several different lengths and actions, depending on the size of fish you plan to chase. Line size can range from 2- to 8-pound (0.9- to 3.6-kg) monofilament or low-diameter superlines.

For panfish (and small trout) you might choose a 24-inch (61-cm) light-action rod and reel combo spooled with 2- to 4-pound-test (0.9- to 1.8-kg) line. In some states, including Minnesota, anglers can use two lines when ice fishing, so I often rig one with a slip-bobber and rig the other rod with a split-shot and #10 teardrop.

Small trout are fished for in much the same manner as you use when fishing for panfish. You can use the same rigs mentioned in the previous paragraphs. The only difference in bait may be the trout species' affinity to brightly colored baits such as the PowerBait® products from Berkley. These come in several forms including pre-formed pellets, grubs and in a paste that can be formed around your hook. In many circumstances, these man-made baits will out-

produce traditional live baits. The other main difference when fishing for small trout is that they suspend in the water column and are fairly nomadic in their movements. Fishing with a locator is a must, to see where the fish are. Be sure to change the depth you are fishing your bait at often. I like to start with the bait several feet (meters) off the bottom and move up in 2-

foot (60-cm) increments until you reach the surface. Also remember that many states have special regulations on trout and you should check them thoroughly prior to your trip.

Larger fish species such as northern pike, lake trout and walleyes can also be caught using a tip-up. This style of fishing allows you to cover large areas effectively, particu-

larly if you are one of a group of anglers. It also allows for trying several different baits at the same time, to quickly determine what the fish want. A tip-up is nothing more than a device to hold line and signal you when a fish takes your bait. Landing a fish on a tip-up is hand-to-hand combat and it often takes a little time to perfect your hook-setting and landing techniques.

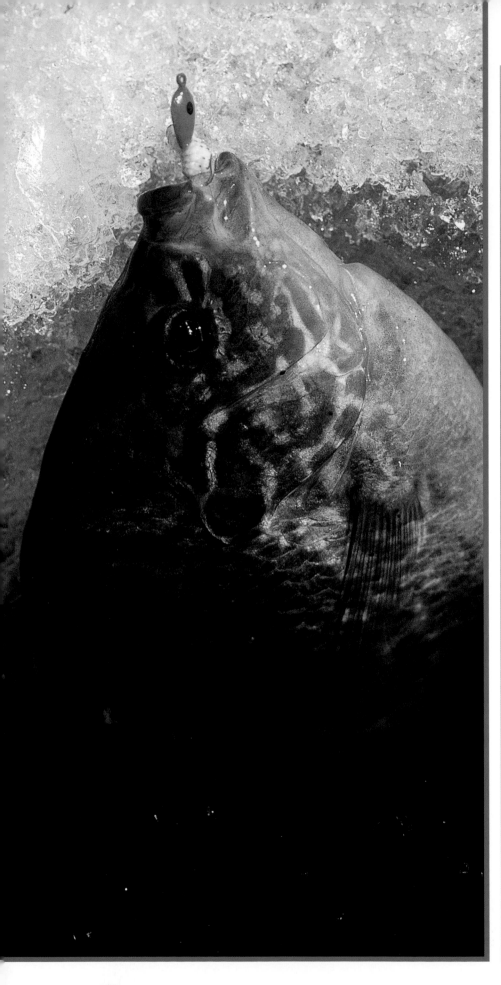

Panfish

Sunfish spend most of the winter roaming weedy flats with a hard bottom near the same areas they spawn in the spring. You can tip your slip-bobber rig with a waxworm and use the smaller larvae on the split-shot rig. Set the slip-bobber line 18 inches (45 cm) off the bottom, open the bail and set it in a rod holder or on the floor of your shelter.

Use the rod with the split-shot rig to work the entire water column from top to bottom. Sunfish often suspend in the water, depending on weather and water clarity. It is critical to have your bait above the fish so they can see it changing depths. Slowly work the bait at different depths until you figure out the depth the fish are holding in.

A flasher-style fish locator rigged for ice fishing eliminates the guesswork. If you have access to one of these units, be sure to charge the battery and bring it along—it could increase the number of fish you catch by 200 percent. I am confident in saying that anglers correctly using a depth finder in the winter cannot be out-fished by an angler without one!

Crappies often suspend over sunken islands and rocky reefs in the winter, often in very large schools. You can use the same rod and rig as you used for sunfish; just switch the bait to a crappie minnow. When crappies are in a negative mood, switch back to larvae and a smaller ice fly. Try hooking on two or three larvae on one hook for crappies that do not want to bite.

A typical ice-fishing rig for sunfish is 4-pound-test (1.8-kg) mono-line with #10 and smaller hooks, teardrop lures or ice flies suspended below a tiny, fixed bobber. Hook waxworms or Eurolarvae onto the lure. Adding small split-shot makes the rig neutrally balanced to show the slightest bite.

Keep a good bend in the rod
while fighting crappies, or for that matter, any species of fish. If you give crappies slack line, the hook may slip out.

When ice fishing keep your gear compact and mobile. This helps you be able to cover several areas in one day while searching for fish. When learning a new lake this may require you to drill fifty-plus holes before catching a fish. GPS units combined with maps that have longitude and latitude lines marked on them and a good flasher unit help find structure quickly.

Trout

In lakes stocked with rainbows and browns, main-lake structure, such as large points and inside turns, is the best place to start. You can stick to the same program but tip your slip-bobber rig with a small fathead or crappie minnow. Stocked trout in lakes can grow to be 5 or 6 pounds (2.3 or 2.7 kg) so 4- to 6-pound-test (1.8- to 2.7-kg) is a good choice when fishing waters known to have larger trout.

One clue to help decide which reel to buy is to slowly turn the drag knob and see if it makes little clicking noises. Although reels with this feature often cost more money, those little clicking noises mean the drag can be adjusted in fine increments, which is critical in the winter. Many ultralight reels do not have this feature and without it your drag can slowly tighten up when fish make long runs. This puts extra pressure on the line, causing it to break or the hook to be pulled from the fish's mouth.

Trout in the winter put up a good fight after being hooked, so be sure to set your drag accordingly. To test your drag, simply grab the line at the end of the rod and pull on it so the rod bends fully. Just before you feel the line has reached its limit, the drag should release. Once you're at this point, back the drag off 1/3 of a turn.

Ice fishing for lake trout in the Great Lakes area and in Canada requires heavier tackle. Lake trout weighing 10 to 20 pounds (4.5 to 9 kg) are not uncommon and can make burning runs. Lakers often suspend in 30 to 40 feet (9 to 12 m) of water over depths of 100 feet

(30 m) or more during the winter. They also suspend over structure like rock humps in depths of 50 to 60 feet (15 to 18 m). Using a 10-inch (25-cm) gas auger gives you more room to fight bigger fish and get their head turned up through the hole.

When lakers make long runs your line takes a real beating on the bottom of the ice hole. The larger hole size reduces the angle of the line at the bottom of the hole; this puts less stress on the line and increases the odds of landing large fish.

The rod of choice is a 36-inch (91-cm) medium-heavy-action spinning or baitcasting rod and reel combo spooled with 8- to 12-pound (3.6- to 5.4-kg) superline. Superlines have little stretch and when you're fishing in 50 feet (15 m) of water, line stretch is not good. They also resist abrasion and stay supple even in cold weather. Most wintertime lakers can be fooled by jigging a 1/2- to 1-ounce (14- to 28-g) bucktail jig tipped with a dead alewife, smelt or sucker meat strip.

Fishing for lakers is much easier with a fish locator, because lakers can come into the area below your hole at any depth and if you're jigging below them they won't see the bait. When a fish is indicated on the flasher unit, slowly raise or lower the jig to directly above the fish. Then experiment with different jigging patterns to see what mood they're in that day. I like to use scent on my jig also, and I've found that the bucktail hair holds scent longer than plastic bodies do.

A tip-up can be your second line and is the most successful when rigged with a live ciscoe. Ciscoes can be caught on most lake trout lakes using the same gear you use for panfish.

A nice brook trout taken through the ice.

Rigs and lures for trout include (1) live-bail hook with split-shot, (2) Rat Finke, (3) caddis, (4) airplane jig, (5) bucktail jig.

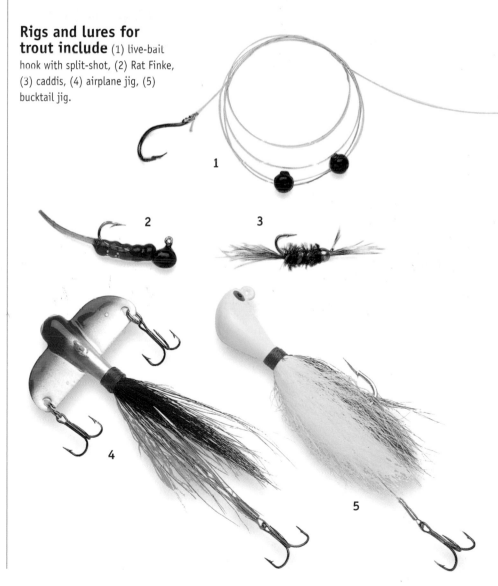

Northern Pike and Bass

Northern pike and bass can be caught using a rod and reel but most anglers (including myself) prefer to set up tip-ups on shallow, weedy flats. I prefer to fish weed flats with a hard bottom, which causes weeds to

grow in clumps and leave openings or lanes for fish to cruise in search of food. After you drill a hole, clear the ice, then look into the hole to make sure the area below it is clear of weeds. (You may need to use your jacket to block the sun to see down into the hole.) If a clump of weeds is below the hole, drill a different hole. Fish need to be able to see your bait to eat it

and if your minnow gets tangled in the weeds, the fish can't see it.

Rig your tip-up with 30-pound (13.5-kg) Dacron line and tie on a steel leader for pike and a 10-pound-test (4.5-kg) leader for bass. Pinch a #4 split-shot on the mono leader and a #2 hook tipped with a small sucker, golden shiner or fathead minnow. On the steel leader pinch on a #4 split-shot and a #1 hook, tipped with a medium to large sucker or lake shiner. (My experience has been that lake shiners out-produce golden shiners for pike.)

Set your tip-ups so the bait is 1½ feet (46 cm) off the bottom. Make as little noise as possible when setting tip-ups on a shallow flat as fish under the ice can hear you—they can even hear you approaching the tip-ups after the flag has popped up. Spread your tip-ups across the weedy flat you are fishing and don't be afraid to move to different depths throughout the day.

Another method for targeting pike in particular, is to use a dead bait or store-bought herring fished right on the bottom with a quick-strike rig. Frozen herring are available at most grocery stores and have worked well for me many times. There is no data on exactly why this presentation is effective. However, it seems to work the best late in the season and it is believed that pike may be feeding on bait that has died through the winter and has collected on the bottom.

If there is a difference in targeting largemouth bass it is that they are often found closer to the outside edge of the flat, near the first break to deeper water. If you are targeting largemouth and the flat is not producing fish, try to locate your tip-ups near the edge. Also keep in mind that largemouth often school in these areas and once you locate fish it is not uncommon to catch several from the same hole. I also like to downsize my hook slightly for largemouth. A #2 live bait hook through a lively shiner often does the trick for me.

Using a Tip-up for Pike

Set the flag arm under the T-shaped spindle after lowering your bait to the desired depth (left). For walleye fishing, set the arm under the smooth side of the spindle so it will trip easily. Set the arm under the grooved side for northern pike fishing with large minnows. A bite is signaled by a tripped flag (below left). You can tell how fast a fish is moving with your bait by how fast the spindle is turning (inset). If the spindle isn't turning, gently pull on the line until you feel resistance. Set the hook with a sharp snap of your wrist (below right).

Walleye and Perch

I spend a lot of time fishing for walleyes and perch in the winter. I start fishing for them on 10- to 15-foot (3- to 4.5-m) rock flats and humps in early winter, then I follow them out to depths of 20 feet (6 m) or more as the season progresses.

Perch bite any bait dropped down a hole when they are feeding, but when they get finicky, use a #8 glow-in-the-dark teardrop tipped with a small crappie minnow or larva. A size BB split-shot gets the bait down to the bottom; perch are typically found within 3 feet (1 m) of the bottom.

As far as rod and reel choice goes, I use the same one I use for crappies and sunfish. Walleyes are often caught in the same areas as perch, and do bite on your perch gear. But if walleyes are your main target use a medium-light 3-foot (1-m) rod and a spinning reel spooled with 6-pound (2.7-kg) monofilament. It is easier to catch perch on a rod that is a little too heavy than risk losing a double-digit-weight walleye on a rod that's too light. Tie a 1½-inch (3.8-cm) jigging spoon directly to the line and tip it with a whole fathead or just the minnow head. Use a knife or scissors to cut the fathead just behind the gills and then penetrate just one of the hooks through both lips.

In low-light conditions use a glow-in-the-dark jig and a small flashlight to charge up the glow paint. Gold-colored spoons accented with chartreuse or orange seem to be effective.

Because walleyes are almost always related to the bottom, you should keep your bait within 4 feet (1.2 m) of the bottom.

Again, a good locator is invaluable for spotting fish that are inspecting your bait. In states where multiple lines are legal, you can set a tip-up away from where you are fishing. Choose to set your tip-up at a different depth than you are fishing; you can use the same rig you use for largemouth bass, a plain #2 or #4 with a fathead or small shiner.

Another favorite technique I use when it is really cold or windy is to have two holes drilled about 3 feet (1 m) apart in my house and have a bobber line in the hole next to the one I am jigging in. Because I generally use a minnow head only while I am jigging, I use a live minnow on a plain hook or single-hook spoon on the bobber line. Oftentimes, sluggish fish will take a live minnow after they were attracted to the area by the jigging spoon, but would not bite it.

When fishing for perch or walleyes with jigs, you can use just the head of a minnow, or a whole minnow (inset). The extra scent created by using only the head often draws strikes.

Chapter 6

How to Get to the Fish

The one thing that seems to be a common thread with serious live-bait anglers is they do whatever it takes to get their bait in the water! No matter how you do it, here are a few tips I have learned over the years—mostly through trial and error.

From Shore

When most people think of shore fishing they get the picture in their minds of riding their bikes to the local lake to fish for panfish, bullheads and carp. This is how I got started, but over the years I have learned a great deal from many veteran anglers who spend a lot of time fishing from shore. It's the oldest and simplest form of fishing.

Shore anglers do not have to contend with long lines at the

HOW TO GET TO THE FISH

Fishing from shore can be quite successful if the surface temperature is below 60°F (15°C). A likely spot is near a dam, where fish tend to congregate. Shore fishing for salmon (inset) peaks in fall, as the fish begin looking for a tributary in which to spawn. As spawning time nears, salmon lose their silvery sheen and turn brownish.

boat launch, the threat of mechanical failure, or the various laws for angling from some type of watercraft.

Many secret fishing spots are easier to access from shore and, when fishing shallow water in the spring and fall, can be more productive when anglers fish from shore. Fishing from shore can be as simple as casting a worm and bobber on a weekend afternoon while listening to the ball game. Maximizing your shore fishing adventure requires a little more preparation to increase the odds of a successful and safe outing.

• Wear waders to land big fish without harming them and to help you retrieve snagged lures.

• Use a Y-branch as a rod holder to keep your rod propped up and free from debris that may cause the reel to malfunction.

• To detect strikes sooner, strike indicators like bells and buzzers help.

• Wear drab-colored clothing when fishing shallow, clear water.

• Bring lightweight folding chairs for comfort.

• Chum the area to be fished a few days beforehand, to attract larger numbers of fish.

• Use headlamps and lanterns when fishing at night to safely fight fish and retie rigs as needed.

• Wear a life jacket when fishing alone, near moving water and during the spring and fall when water temperatures are cold and hypothermia is possible.

• Try wading out to your waist before casting. It will add distance to each cast and may help you reach the deeper water where the fish are holding.

Wading

Trout, bass and salmon are just three species that may require you to get into the water and wade to the fish to be more productive. Wading can be done with or without waders, depending on water temperatures and creatures (such as bloodsuckers and chiggers) that live in a given body of water. I do a great deal of wade-fishing and I prefer the security of a comfortable pair of waders and wading shoes. The ability to wade allows me to fish areas that may not be accessible by land due to no-trespassing laws.

Many states in the Upper Midwest allow anglers to roam freely if they keep their feet in the water while fishing along the shoreline. Being in the water with the fish gives me a feeling of being connected to the body of water. Wading, unlike shore fishing, gives you the chance to cover more water in search of fish. I like to wade while fishing in lakes and reservoirs, around channels, inlets or outlets and swimming beaches at night. Wade-fishing tends to be the most productive when fish are shallow in the spring and fall.

• Use baby powder inside your waders, which allows your feet to slip in much easier.

• Wear felt-soled wading shoes and those with screw-in cleats to reduce slippage on moss-covered rocks.

• Slide your feet slowly along the bottom rather than stepping, when wading over uneven terrain.

• Use a wading staff to steady yourself when crossing fast current or deep water. You can purchase one or make your own from a 2- to 3-inch-diameter (5- to 7.6-cm) dead tree limb found along the shore.

• Seek out and collect bait that may be living along the shoreline under rocks, logs and muddy grass banks.

• When fishing shallow water move along slowly and make as little noise as possible. Fish can sense vibration from footsteps and ripples on the water, which may spook them into deeper water.

• Use the buddy system to safely make deep-water and fast-current crossings.

• Always dry your waders after use.

Wading gives you more mobility than simply fishing from shore. This strategy allows you to fish deeper water and land fish easier.

Canoes make it practical to fish lakes and streams that are otherwise inaccessible. A canoe's light weight also makes it relatively easy to portage between lakes.

Canoe

Living in Minnesota I have the opportunity to visit the Boundary Waters Canoe Area Wilderness. This is a large series of lakes and portages set aside by the state for primitive recreation. Restrictions prohibit the use of any gas-operated machinery inside the BWCAW, so canoes are used to transport camping and fishing gear. Throughout high school and college a canoe was perfect for me because all I needed was a car to transport my canoe, which I could store alongside the house when the garage was full. Canoes are great for accessing small lakes, farm ponds and floating streams or rivers. And they are a great alternative to a boat, which may require a hitch system, trailer and large engine to haul them.

Canoes are much quieter than gas-powered boats and allow you to sneak up on fish in shallow water without being detected. Canoes also provide a great workout when you paddle across a larger lake into a headwind, loaded down with gear—you will feel the burn the next day! There's something magical about fishing from a canoe; after all, it's what helped the earliest anglers evolve their strategies from shore fishing and wade-fishing.

- Bring a rope and a small mesh bag that can be filled with rocks for an anchor.
- Use PVC pipe tied to the supports of the canoe to store rods when portaging, to free your hands to carry other gear.
- Use a portable depth finder to locate structure.
- Stabilize your canoe with outriggers when fishing larger water.
- Reduce stress to the lower back with backrest seats.
- When crossing open-water areas or paddling to the next portage, you can row-troll with a slip-sinker rig fished on the bottom to catch your lunch.
- When fishing with a friend, take turns fishing and steadying the canoe in windy conditions.

Float tubes work well for getting access to remote locations, and also give you mobility to fish in deeper water away from shore.

Float Tube and Kick Boat

Float tubes have been available for about fifteen years. They were first used out West where anglers could backpack them into remote mountain lakes to fish for trout. As their popularity grew they began selling throughout the country and many shops stocked several styles.

A deflated float tube easily fits in a medium-size duffel bag. You can carry it around in the trunk of your car next to the jumper cables and spare tire.

I like to use waders when I float; they keep the creatures off of my legs and keep my legs warm when fishing in the cool waters of spring and fall. You sit in a float tube with your legs hanging below you. Just as ducks use their webbed feet, you use flippers to propel the tube along while fishing. Most float tubes are equipped with several large pockets to store gear, food and a rain jacket. Here's a good tip: Avoid using treble hooks when fishing from a float tube because of the risk of poking a hole in the inner tube, especially when landing fish.

Kick boats evolved from float tubes and come equipped with oars, allowing you to cover water quickly. Kick boats have separate pontoons, one on each side. These boats are open in the middle so you wear flippers to steady the boat while fishing. Large pockets are also available for storage of gear.

• Use a shorter-handled rod when fishing from a float tube. Because you're sitting down, a longer handle would hang up in your clothing.

• Mount a portable depth finder to the tube to aid in locating structure.

• When fighting large fish remember to raise your legs when the fish charges the tube. I have lost more than one trophy fish due to it getting wrapped in my legs and flippers.

• Use your legs, not just your ankles and feet, to propel at top speed to cross open areas of water.

• Eat a banana to reduce any leg cramps you may feel while float tubing.

• Do not store your float tube fully inflated in the sun or other hot area; the tube will expand and put stress on the zipper or stitching.

• Wear a life jacket; they are required in many states while float tubing.

• Wear bright colors when fishing lakes with boat traffic; you'll be more visible.

• Use a small anchor tied to a marker buoy to secure the tube in windy conditions or when fishing a small piece of structure.

Boat

When I find myself engaged in a conversation with a fellow angler for the first time, one of the first questions I'm asked is what kind of boat I have. A boat, no matter what size or shape, is a sign of true commitment to the sport of angling in many circles of the fishing world. Owning or having access to a boat allows anglers freedom to fish several different bodies of water for all species of fish, provided there is adequate public access. I use a 16-foot (5-m) jon boat to fish smaller lakes with unimproved accesses and a 20-foot (6-m) bass boat to fish larger lakes.

The first two things to consider when purchasing a boat is whether you have a safe place to store it and whether your vehicle can safely tow it. Your boat will become the home of all of your fishing gear so safe storage is a must to protect your investment. When buying your first boat start small and be sure to get one with adequate horsepower in the back and a big trolling motor in the front if possible. I prefer bunk trailers over roller trailers because a bunk trailer supports the boat better when moving.

I urge you to keep good mental notes on what you like and don't like about various boats you try. This will help you select the boat best suited to your needs when you're ready to buy or trade up.

- Carry two anchors for better positioning over schools of fish and small pieces of structure.
- Use a drift sock to adjust the drifting or trolling speed of your boat.
- If a front-mounted trolling motor is being used, also mount a depth finder up front with the transducer attached to the bottom of the trolling motor. This setup gives you a more precise look at changes in structure.
- Check the propeller on the gas motor often to remove any fishing line or other debris that may have collected around the shaft.
- If your boat doesn't have a bait well, use a cooler and a simple aeration pump to create one.
- Mount some kind of light if you plan to fish at night.
- Use rod holders to make still-fishing and drifting with multiple lines much more enjoyable.
- I also recommend some type of rod holder for your rods when trailering or running with the big motor. You will spend less time untangling rods and more time fishing!

Boats are the perfect choice for carrying a large amount of gear long distances. They also make for safe travel in rough water.

INDEX

Contributing Photographers

Gerald Almy
Maurertown, VA
© Gerald Almy: p. 102

Denver Bryan
Bozeman, MT
© Denver Bryan/
DenverBryan.com: p. 121

Jan Finger
Baxter, MN
© Jan Finger/Red Pine: pp. 3BL,
3BC, 3BR

F. Eugene Hester
Springfield, VA
© F. Eugene Hester: p. 17E

Dwight R. Kuhn
Dexter, ME
© Dwight R. Kuhn: 37C

Bill Lindner Photography
Minneapolis, MN
© Bill Lindner/blpstudio.com:
cover, back cover TR, pp. 4, 6,
7T, 11TR, 17ABCDF, 21T, 21BR,
32, 44, 56, 58, 66, 70, 71C, 82,
83, 88, 89, 90, 104, 109, 111,
112, 113T, 114, 116

Gunnar Miesen
Eden Prairie, MN
© Gunnar Miesen: p. 107

John E. Phillips
Birmingham, AL
© John E. Phillips: pp. 42, 120

David J. Sams
Dallas, TX
© David J. Sams/davidjsams.com:
pp. 3TR, 96

Doug Stamm
Prairie du Sac, WI
© Doug Stamm/stammphoto.com:
back cover BR, pp. 50, 55C, 59,
64, 72, 77, 81B, 120, 122

Illustrator

Jon Q. Wright
Walker, MN
© Jon Q. Wright/Aqua Images: p.
30T

(Note: T=Top, C=Center, B=Bottom,
L=Left, R=Right)

Creative Publishing international
is your complete source of How-to information for the Outdoors.

Available Outdoor Titles:

Hunting Books
- Advanced Turkey Hunting
- Advanced Whitetail Hunting
- Bowhunting Equipment & Skills
- The Complete Guide to Hunting
- Dog Training
- Duck Hunting
- Elk Hunting
- Hunting Record-Book Bucks
- Mule Deer Hunting
- Muzzleloading
- Pronghorn Hunting
- Whitetail Hunting
- Whitetail Techniques & Tactics
- Wild Turkey

Fishing Books
- Advanced Bass Fishing
- The Art of Freshwater Fishing
- The Complete Guide to Freshwater Fishing
- Fishing for Catfish

- Fishing Rivers & Streams
- Fishing Tips & Tricks
- Fishing with Artificial Lures
- Inshore Salt Water Fishing
- Kids Gone Fishin'
- Largemouth Bass
- Modern Methods of Ice Fishing
- Northern Pike & Muskie
- Offshore Salt Water Fishing
- Panfish
- Salt Water Fishing Tactics
- Smallmouth Bass
- Striped Bass Fishing: Salt Water Strategies
- Successful Walleye Fishing
- Trout

Fly Fishing Books
- The Art of Fly Tying
- The Art of Fly Tying – CD ROM
- Fishing Dry Flies – Surface Presentations for Trout in Streams

- Fishing Nymphs, Wet Flies & Streamers – Subsurface Techniques for Trout in Streams
- Fly-Fishing Equipment & Skills
- Fly Fishing for Trout in Streams
- Fly Fishing for Beginners
- Fly-Tying Techniques & Patterns

Cookbooks
- America's Favorite Fish Recipes
- America's Favorite Wild Game Recipes
- Babe & Kris Winkleman's Great Fish & Game Recipes
- Cooking Wild in Kate's Camp
- Cooking Wild in Kate's Kitchen
- Dressing & Cooking Wild Game
- Game Bird Cookery
- The New Cleaning & Cooking Fish
- Preparing Fish & Wild Game
- The Saltwater Cookbook
- Venison Cookery

To purchase these or other Creative Publishing international titles,
contact your local bookseller, or visit our web site at
www.creativepub.com

The Complete
FLY FISHERMAN™